Freedom...

is a Path Book
offering practical spirituality
to enrich everyday living

"Your word is a lamp to my feet
and a light to my path"
Psalm 119:105

From Fear To
Freedom

Abused Wives Find Hope and Healing

Sheila A. Rogers

Path Books
an imprint of ABC Publishing
Anglican Book Centre
600 Jarvis Street
Toronto, Ontario M4Y 2J6

Printed in Canada

Text set in Janson; display set in Papyrus
Cover and text design by Jane Thornton

National Library of Canada Cataloguing in Publication
Rogers, Sheila Ann, 1948-
    From fear to freedom : abused wives find hope and healing /
Sheila A. Rogers.

Includes bibliographical references.
ISBN 1-55126-358-0

1. Wife abuse. 2. Abused wives. I. Title.

HV6626.R64 2002   362.82'92   C2002-902272-X

Contents

Acknowledgements   7

Chapter 1
  Introduction   9
Chapter 2
  What Is Abuse?   14
Chapter 3
  Lily   21
Chapter 4
  Abuse and the Church   31
Chapter 5
  Marie   44
Chapter 6
  The Seven S's of Staying   52
Chapter 7
  Barbara   68
Chapter 8
  The Five L's of Leaving   76
Chapter 9
  Opal   88
Chapter 10
  Hope for Healing   97
Chapter 11
  Shirley   119
Chapter 12
  Where Are They Today?   128

Appendix A
  Boundaries   131
Appendix B
  Family Rules and Roles   135
Appendix C
  Post-Traumatic Stress Disorder   140
Appendix D
  Defence Mechanisms   143
Appendix E
  The Cycle of Violence   146
Appendix F
  Recommended Reading   148
References   150

Acknowledgements

This book represents a collaborative effort by many people, each contributing their own unique ideas and experiences. I would like to list all those who shared their ideas, expertise, and energy. However, in order to protect the anonymity of those mentioned in these pages, I have chosen to refrain from identifying specific contributors.

I wish to offer my sincere appreciation to all those involved. I am extremely grateful to colleagues who encouraged me to produce the book, to those who offered professional expertise, and to colleagues, neighbours, and friends who read and critiqued early drafts of the manuscript. I have been fortunate to receive great support and encouragement from the editorial staff at ABC Publishing. I especially appreciate the support of my family, who liberally offered patience, affirmation, and inspiration.

The book would not have been possible, however, without the help of five women who courageously shared their journeys. I owe a debt of gratitude to these women for the confidence they expressed in my ability to present their stories, and their willingness to entrust me with the intimate details of their lives.

Chapter 1

Introduction

Barbara's voice echoes through a church auditorium. She sings with the feeling of someone who has known the sorrow of mourning and the joy of freedom. For decades there was no joy in her life, but now she laughs as the audience embraces her. After twenty years of married life with a man who criticized, scorned, and hit her, the woman who once came close to taking her own life is undergoing a remarkable transformation.

Barbara is typical of a group of women about whom we are just learning. Although family violence has been studied extensively over the last two decades and studies show that many abused wives hold some form of religious views, only recently has research been conducted on Christian women who are exposed to some form of psychological or physical oppression in their marriages. Isolated in their congregations and bound by shame, many feel unable to share their pain in the church, the place we would believe to be safest. The abuse often goes unrecognized by church members and unchallenged by the church.

In the United States and Canada, wife abuse is reaching epidemic proportions — between 30 per cent and 60 per cent of wives in the US according to studies cited by Nancy Nason-Clark (1997). A Statistics Canada study mentioned by Nason-Clark indicates that three in ten Canadian women have experienced at least one incident of physical or sexual abuse by their partner. Wife abuse occurs among church people at about the same rate as in society at large. What makes this information startling is that abuse of any kind is so much at variance with the law of love that forms the basis of the gospels.

This book evolved from a conviction that church communities need more information about, and heightened awareness of, the insidious nature of wife abuse. The research that laid the foundation for this work focused on the experiences of wives who endured abuse and mistreatment and yet maintained their Christian beliefs. The project looked at values, meanings, and spiritual growth in relation to the experience of being abused. Much of the initial work centred on examining the role of Christian theology in supporting and perpetuating certain attitudes toward marriage, divorce, and wife abuse. The body of the study involved interviews with eight women, of whom five are presented here. The picture that unfolds in these pages shows hope and transformation. Analysis of the patterns and themes that emerged revealed a comprehensive picture of a woman who struggles with her identity and faith in a relationship that is destroying her, and finally breaks through into a new life.

The women whose stories appear in this book all come from backgrounds that can be described as "conservative evangelical" Christian. Conservative evangelicals place great emphasis on the authority of the Bible, and many are inclined to understand the Bible literally. They are likely to consider that its words delineate precise rules for living. Consequently, since several passages in the Bible treat marriage as a life-long sacred contract, they conclude that divorce is inadmissible. The women in this book, and many others like them, feel bound to their marriages no matter how abusive they are. Some even interpret the abuse as a means by which God tests or teaches them.

However, the experience of the women in this book cannot be dismissed as a peculiarly conservative evangelical problem. It is not long since the whole church was at least officially inflexible in teaching that marriage is invariably indissoluble. The Roman Catholic Church still does not permit divorce and remarriage. Other mainline churches are somewhat cautious about both, but have developed guidelines that make allowances where marriages have, to all intents and purposes, broken down. In actual practice, many Roman Catholic clergy and lay people tacitly accept divorces and second marriages made outside the church, and it is quite likely that similar allowances are made in many conservative evangelical congregations. But even when the church's official rules change, old attitudes may persist and continue to give pain to divorced or remarried people. In Chapter Four we will consider some of the theological and disciplinary issues surrounding divorce — and abuse.

The focus of this book is on husbands abusing wives. It does not intend to suggest that wives do not abuse husbands. Many of the comments made about abuse and abusive marriages in this book can also be applied where men are abused by women.

From Fear to Freedom follows the lives of five women as they move from childhood into marriage and ultimately back out of it. Since they were bound by their care for men who mistreated them and confused by their relationships with a God who failed to change their marriages, the book also documents each individual's spiritual journey. The reader witnesses their anguish, despair, courage, humour, hope, and rebirth. Each woman selected a pseudonym and produced a phrase that summarized her journey. Some factual details of the stories have been changed to protect anonymity, but these changes in no way alter the core of the stories or influence the findings of the study.

Lily lived for nearly twenty years with a man who possessed a violent temper, broke household items, and verbally abused her.

Marie was first married at seventeen to a man who broke her bones and almost killed her. At twenty three, she married again, this time to a man who used extreme psychological control to intimidate her.

Barbara's husband physically abused her, even in front of her children and their friends.

Opal spent close to twenty years in a marriage to a needy man who drank excessively and pursued other women.

Shirley was emotionally abused by the husband who gave her four children and then told them that she was a terrible mother.

From Fear to Freedom elucidates the experience of each woman as she embarks on a journey toward healing, guided by her relationship with God, her unique personality characteristics, and her specific life situation. It provides validation for Christian women who have been abused, and assists those who are currently suffering, to find and begin a healing journey. It offers practical suggestions and ideas, not only for wounded women to heal but also for the Christian community to play a role in the healing process.

Interspersed among the five portraits are discussions of wife abuse in a cultural and religious context. The book identifies and examines different forms of abuse, and the dynamics of relationships in which violence, both physical and emotional, occurs. It traces attitudes toward women from biblical times to the present and considers religious ideologies in relation to the roles of men and women. The patterns and themes that emerge in the women's stories are grouped into two major categories: those factors that contributed to tolerance of the abuse and those that led to a decision to leave the marriage.

The abused woman can be anyone in your church: the person with whom you car pool to Bible study, your child's Sunday school teacher, the minister's wife. Or she may be you! The telling may at times be painful, yet ultimately the stories are of transformation. This book aims to offer hope and healing to those who are abused, and to set the captives free.

Chapter 2

What Is Abuse?

"He made a fist and punched me in the head."
"He threatened to kill me and then commit suicide."
"He often belittled me, telling me I was lazy and had no self-discipline."

This chapter is intended to help church people identify and name abuse in order that they can support victims. Recognizing abuse is the first step.

Recent years have seen many changes both within the church and outside it. The greater willingness of women to report abuse and talk openly about it has facilitated a new understanding and awareness. Nonetheless, shame, embarrassment, guilt, and fear have kept many women, including Christian women, from sharing their plight. Many who are being abused do not even realize what is happening to them, and when seeking help and answers, they are met with judgement and condemnation by well-meaning but misguided friends, advisors, and even ministers and priests.

Abuse within the confines of marriage can take many forms,

but it falls into two broad categories: physical and emotional. Although there has been a proliferation of material on wife abuse, defining and naming the violence that occurs within marriage continues to be a difficult and sensitive task. Wife abuse has emerged within a historical social and religious context that makes women vulnerable. The ancient partriarchal assumption that the man has the right and duty to control his wife has been perpetuated until recently, partly with the help of the church. Even now, as both rules and attitudes change, the church population, in common with the wider population, is not always able to identify and recognize abuse. Only in recent years have Christians become aware of the extent to which women in the churches they attend are subjected to abuse at the hands of their husbands. This is quite alarming since,

> the drama and tragedy of wife abuse will touch most of us at some point in our lives. Whether or not we are abused ourselves, or have been raised in an abusive family, at some time in our lives we are almost certainly going to come into close contact with someone who has (Barnett and LaViolette, 1993, xvi).

Marital abuse includes all forms of violent or abusive behaviour that occur within the intimate confines of marriage. Although we can recognize deliberate acts of physical violence, other abusive behaviour includes willful neglect, sexual abuse, emotional abuse, financial abuse, and threats of intended aggressive acts. Beverly Engel (1990) describes abuse as "any behaviour that is designed to control or subjugate another human being through the use of fear, humiliation, and verbal or physical assaults."

Engel asserts that "a great proportion of the damage caused

by physical or sexual abuse is emotional," while Melissa Miller (1994) claims that physical abuse always includes emotional abuse. She identifies physical abuse as any behaviour that injures another, regardless of whether or not there are bones broken or internal injuries. She lists these behaviours: hitting, burning, slapping, pinching, whipping, biting, and the destruction of property or pets. Two other researchers, James and Phyllis Alsdurf, also add: scratching, stabbing, shooting, and raping (1989, p. 29).

Emotional abuse, according to Engel, includes a wide range of behaviours "from verbal abuse and constant criticism to more subtle tactics such as intimidation, manipulation, and the refusal to ever be pleased." Emotional abuse, she says, is a form of brainwashing that gradually cuts to the core of an individual and insidiously wears away the victim's self-concept so that, "eventually the recipient of the abuse loses all sense of self and all remnants of personal value." The insidious nature of emotional abuse is reflected in the fact that the abuser's behaviour is not always obvious and the immediate impact is not dramatic. It creates a constant climate of confusion that keeps a woman believing she is trapped and that there is no way out. It deprives her of confidence and prevents her from defining what is happening to her. The following list compiled by Amy Wildman White (1993) includes many behaviours that constitute emotional abuse:

1. manipulative and heavy-handed tactics eliciting fear, guilt, pity, or anger
2. intimidation
3. making a person feel vulnerable, in danger, unprotected, or helpless

4. put-downs, criticism, verbal abuse
5. causing shame or humiliation
6. controlling another's schedule
7. keeping another ignorant regarding herself, the world, finances or others
8. keeping a person in crisis, thus off balance and occupied
9. conspiracy and turning others away from aiding the person
10. creating situations in which there is no way to win
11. lying or gossip
12. threatening self-harm or suicide; possessiveness and jealousy

In her book, *The Emotionally Abused Woman*, Beverly Engel presents an alternative list of emotionally abusive behaviours:

1. Domination: taking control of all aspects of another person's life, *e.g.*, money, social life.
2. Verbal assaults: berating, belittling, criticizing, name-calling, screaming, threatening, blaming, using sarcasm and humiliation.
3. Abusive expectations: unreasonable demands to satisfy his needs such as undivided attention, frequent sex, or requiring his spouse to spend all her free time with him. No matter how much she gives, it is never enough.
4. Emotional blackmail: coercion by fear, guilt, or compassion, such as threatening to end a relationship, rejecting her, or distancing her.
5. Unpredictable responses: inconsistent responses such as drastic mood swings or sudden emotional outbursts for no apparent reason. He says one thing one day and the opposite the next.

6. Constant criticism: unrelenting criticism of his spouse, always finding fault, and unable ever to be pleased. She becomes convinced that nothing she does is good enough.
7. Character assassination: he blows her mistakes out of proportion, gossips about her past failures, humiliates or criticizes, makes fun of her in front of others, or discounts her successes.
8. Gas lighting: using insidious techniques to make another person doubt their perception and memory, *e.g.*, denying that certain events occurred, accusing her of lying or exaggerating.
9. Constant chaos: continual upheavals, starting arguments, creating conflict, negative moods.
10. Sexual harassment: unwelcome sexual advances or verbal conduct of a sexual nature. Pressuring a woman to become sexual against her will.

The effects of the abuse manifest as fear, depression, low self-esteem, inability to trust, difficulty being comfortable in social situations, and physical symptoms such as nausea and dizziness. A woman feels like a child in the relationship because she has to ask permission or apologize for her behaviour. She feel powerless or "less than" her mate. She stops seeing friends and family because her partner criticizes them. She believes that she is to blame for her mate's behaviour and feels responsible for the relationship and making it work.

Relationships in which abuse occurs are characterized by certain dynamics that reflect intense attachment between partners. The attachment does not allow partners to develop their own individuality, but keeps each spouse preoccupied with what the partner does. The husband in such a relationship is often possessive and dependent and feels that he is incomplete, inadequate, or unable to live without the other person. The wife, who also depends on her husband for her significance and her identity, feels that she too cannot live without him. The husband uses intimidation to control his wife and to keep her bound to him. As these behaviours increase in intensity, so too does her need for positive reinforcement from him.

The Cycle of Violence, first identified by Walker (1979) develops as a result of this intensity and dependency (Appendix E, p. 146). This cycle involves three phases: *tension building*, in which the tension intensifies; *escalation of tension*, when the abuse occurs; and *contrition*, during which the abuser expresses remorse. The cycle actually increases the wife's dependency and reinforces her hope that her husband will become more loving. With each repetition she becomes more dependent on the abuser and more locked into the hope that he will change. The woman's responses have been referred to as "learned helplessness" (Barnett and LaViolette, 1993) because the Cycle of Violence induces a type of psychological paralysis in which the woman believes that she is helpless to control the events of her life. When she stays long enough in a situation of perceived helplessness, she is likely to give up entirely and accept the circumstances, including the abuse.

In order to recover and heal, a woman experiencing abuse needs to break free and move to a place of strength. If she is able to do this, she forces the husband either to change or to lose the marriage (Wildman White, 1993). Most men who exhibit abusive behaviours are not likely to change until the cost of not changing is too great. Then, at least in some cases, the man will do whatever it takes to save the marriage. The stories in this book are about women who became strong, but whose husbands chose to lose their marriages rather than seek help to change.

Increased understanding will make it possible for Christians to be part of the community that helps to save women from abuse and sometimes to save marriages. Transforming abuse into honour and respect gives honour and respect also to God.

Chapter Three

Lily

*"I was weary from trying so hard,
for so long, to feel safe
in dangerous places."*

R eligious radio programs provided the backdrop for a childhood that consisted of farm work, regular church attendance, and Christian school education. I was the third of six
children born into this very strict religious family. Chicken
chores and church. I learned early on to be dutiful, hardworking,
and self-effacing. Our home was not a harmonious place; my
parents argued much of the time and my father exerted his control by shouting orders with a booming voice. We children were
often drawn into our parents' fights. Each parent would try to
win us to their side. Various coalitions would unite with mother
against the injustice of father's behaviour. We all felt sorry for
our mother, who usually bore the brunt of father's ravings. Despite the anger shown by our parents, we were not allowed to
express anger, and if we did, we were belted, usually by my father. Whenever we were in public, especially at church, our
parents appeared entirely different: they presented to the world
a congenial and harmonious face.

We all worked hard on the farm, and even harder to earn
our parents' acceptance, but I always had the feeling that I was

never good enough. My mother was always too weary to play with the children. I wanted my father's love, but it too seemed elusive, and my mother resented my attempts to win it. My father remained distant from the family by choosing swing shifts at a factory and sleeping during the daytime, by seldom showing affection and being ever ready to criticize. My mother, like her children, repeatedly tried to win his approval. Her deepening despair and anger contaminated every relationship among the eight of us, causing distance, detachment, and dishonesty for decades.

When I reached my teen years, I felt deep sadness about life. I longed to escape the family and meet others, but my parents forbade me to form friendships, respond to dating invitations, or pursue my own interests. I remember watching other people and wondering if they felt as lonely as I did. Finally at eighteen, I did escape from my parents' home; I was sent to a strict residential Bible college. At the start of my first academic year, I met a fellow student. I became infatuated with this young man, the first friendship of my choosing.

Al swept me off my feet with promises and fantasies, and I loved it. I had always had to prove that I was worthy of being loved, but Al appeared to accept me right away, even though it was against the rules on this religious campus to speak or meet at any time. I thought he was brave and daring to take such risks for me, and for once I felt important to someone. When Al asked me to quit school after one and a half years to marry him, I quickly agreed. I now realize that I married him out of rebellion against all the rules and joyless traditions of family and school.

Two months after the wedding the problems began. Al began to shout and criticize me. Small occurrences such as burning toast would cause him to explode verbally, yelling that I was stupid and inadequate, and bombing my self-esteem. Al blamed my parents' marriage for my inability to be the wife he wanted, but I was never able to figure out what kind of wife he really did want. Things quickly worsened. If I failed to please, Al would throw cherished items at the walls or kick down a door. Then he would drive away angrily, tires screeching. The following day, he'd return bringing flowers, food treats, and tearful promises that it would not happen again. I always verbally forgave him to end the crisis, but the same thing would happen again and again.

We were usually strapped for money, since Al was unable to keep a job because of his temper. Our financial difficulties meant we had to move for him to find more work. We moved quite a bit. In spite of the moves, we were very active in the many churches we attended. We were often involved in church leadership and would sing together for church concerts. My love of music brought me plenty of affirmation from others, which temporarily strengthened my shattered self-esteem.

We had three children quite soon after we were married: John, David, and Hannah. Following their births the abuse escalated, and they became additional targets for Al's wrath. Nothing the children did was exempt from his critical eye. Their clothes, friends, and even breakfast cereal were subjected to ridicule. He would mock and jeer when I shared tender moments with them. A hug for Hannah or a kiss for John or David would be met with shouts so loud it would send the children sobbing to their rooms. His jealousy of my affection for our three children sabotaged our home life. In addition, Al verbally and emotionally sabotaged my mothering strengths, causing me deep unnecessary guilt as a parent.

Friends and neighbours began to notice, because his ill treatment of us was no longer confined to the privacy of home. I was often aware of the curious stares and averted eyes of passers-by, pitying us but offering no refuge or intervention for our safety. Even my in-laws expressed concern. In fact, Al's father and sister suggested that I leave him, offering assistance with babysitting and financial help. However, I had been taught that marriage is for life and that I must stay at all costs or I "would go to hell," as one shouting angry minister warned me after my first attempt to leave the marriage.

Alone in a sea of confusion, I struggled to keep afloat, often calling out to God to change Al and restore our family. Numerous prayer requests shared in church, and tearful altar-call collapses, achieved no shift in our relationship. Nothing changed. A paralysing numbness crept into my mind and spirit. Deep inside I would weep in the dark when I could not sleep. I'd grieve for myself, my parents, my children, and all the hurt in the world. I woke often after one of Al's episodes with tears falling onto my pillow in the middle of a disturbing dream. I called it "The Pain" and tried to run from it by getting lost in the frenzied busyness of work and volunteering in church and school.

Despite my best efforts, I grew more depressed and desperate. I decided to seek help from a pastor. Several pastors from various denominations agreed to counsel us, but Al would go to one session and refuse to go again. None of the pastors seemed equipped to provide guidance or help to us. In fact, instead of helping, several of them made shocking sexual advances toward me! When I was twenty-two, our minister used the "counselling hour" to detail his struggle between an affair and his duty to his wife and the church. In another city five years later, I remember screaming, "How can you do this?" at the minister who had just served communion and now, following the service, under pretence of arranging music for the evening service, wanted a sexual response from me. His reply was, "But God brought you into my life because he knew my wife wasn't meeting my needs." When I was thirty-two, one of our pastors threatened my very faith by warning, "If you go out from the covering of this church, your marriage will never last," as if attendance alone would prevent failure. I learned that some religious leaders were no better off than me, hiding pain or loneliness behind busy smiling masks of religious service.

My struggle became so painful that just attending church triggered unhappy memories. I experienced worsening health problems like digestive disorders, breathing difficulties, and painful monthly cycles. My feelings of isolation at church were now exacerbated as I fended off sexual advances from clergy or parishioners who knew of my vulnerability. My relationship with my earthly father had left me unable to embrace the father image of God, so I began to spend more time praying to Jesus and reading the Bible. I could relate to the image of Jesus as a friend. I desperately needed to relate to the Jesus who could be my rescuer and saviour. I had always loved music, but the years of accumulated sorrow had choked my desire to sing with Al when our duets masked the disharmony in our home. But I gradually found that I could absorb the words of songs that spoke of Jesus' mercy and compassion. I turned to him as healer and restorer, the only one who could provide comfort and strength to my woman's soul and make it possible to endure this exhausting marriage. And yet I wondered why Jesus was allowing our cycle of agony to escalate.

I deliberately became less active in church life, because I feared that sharing my experiences with others would make them judge and condemn me as an ungodly wife, that people would accuse me of unforgivable sin, and that Al would become furious should he discover that I had revealed our family secrets to someone in the congregation. Over time, Al's rudeness to my friends drove them away. I stopped inviting them to our home and refused invitations to have coffee or meet for lunch, because Al had accused me of loving my friends more than him. I even neurotically stopped answering the telephone for a time. I was determined to pour all my energy into enduring the marriage, and my pain and damaging beliefs led me to forsake even the friends who urged me to stop trying so hard, and who might have supported me in terminating this cycle of violence.

We continued to move from one town to another, as Al's joblessness and our mounting debts aggravated his resentment of me. I cried out to Jesus, asking him again and again to change Al and to heal all our brokenness. I attempted to initiate discussions with Al about our relationship so that I could understand him better. I began attending counselling sessions with female therapists, working hard to heal my own wounds first. I tried to help Al improve his relationship with the children, but nothing seemed to work, and I just felt more isolated from husband, family, and former friends.

But things got worse. Al sometimes raped me. I kept trying to understand him and to get him to see that what was happening in our marriage reflected childhood injuries in both of us, but this also made him angry. My emotional state deteriorated. I could scarcely look after the children and work my day job. One Saturday, when the children were away visiting relatives and I was sitting in a chair overwhelmed and unable to do even the daily chores, my thoughts strayed to the bottle of muscle relaxant pills in the medicine cabinet. I don't know what happened, but I just got up and took them.

When Al got home in the middle of the day, he found me collapsed on the bed. After a few hours in the hospital, where they asked no questions about my personal life, I was sent home to nurse my invisible pain. A friend invited me to use her home for a short time of rest and recovery. Two weeks away from Al and the children provided me with a change, but still I was unable to share my sorrow and despair with anyone. Bottled up inside were years and years of ridicule, criticism, sarcasm, threats, and violence. I was haunted by fears for the children's safety. I did not know what Al would do to them in my absence, so I returned home and resigned myself to the idea that my unhappiness would continue.

I badly wanted the children to be safe from Al's anger. I implored Jesus to heal and restore my life and my children's lives. But no longer did I ask Jesus to change Al. I stopped trying to save the marriage. I had reached the point where I had nothing left to give. I began to pray fervently, asking Jesus for strength, wisdom, and understanding for myself. In slow motion, over time, my prayers were answered. My eyes, once clouded by fatigue and anxiety, now became able to see the state of the marriage in a way I had not seen it before. I could see how my childhood experiences had crippled me and set me up to marry a man like Al. I could also see how Al's behaviour was a result of difficulties in his family. These insights gained during the counselling sessions made sense, but they did not change the marriage pattern we both felt trapped in.

I kept praying to be rescued, and as time passed I started to feel stronger. As I read books, received counselling, and attended support groups, I received more insights about myself, our relationship, and Al. Inspired by my emerging self-respect, I confronted him with the hypocrisy of our marriage, our church life, and his employment in a religious organization. His immediate response was confusion and indifference regarding solutions; later he handed me a list of thirteen reasons why the marriage breakdown was basically all my fault. This was an important turning point for me. Al's dishonest accusations made the decision easier: I deliberately refused to carry the total blame for the failure of our marriage.

Now, instead of working harder at the marriage, I began preparing for the logical ending. I drew closer to Jesus, the only one I could trust. I began weeping my years of anguish to him in prayerful solitude. I asked him to show me scriptures about mercy after relationship failures.

When I said I wanted out of the marriage, Al's response shocked me. He simply agreed. He seemed to be as relieved as I was. After that things happened quickly. Al moved out, filed for divorce, and stated clearly that he did not want custody of the children. I continued making the mortgage and auto payments from my salary, shared tears of relief with my children, and later signed the divorce papers with a sense of gratitude for my survival. Al left the country to travel, with no forwarding address, while I reassured my children that the new rules in our home were honesty, safety, authenticity, and spiritual freedom.

Unfortunately, the response of the church congregation was negative, but this just reinforced the sense of loss that I had already experienced in the church. I soon discovered that neither I nor the children were comfortable at church activities programmed for intact families, many of which might be hypocritical or living in abusive situations. Gradually we withdrew completely. Jesus, however, did not leave me. His love continued to sustain me. I called out to him to give me strength each day. Realizing my importance to him helped me little by little to gain a sense of myself as being worthwhile.

Relieved to be away from their father, the children started to voice their grief, anger, and confusion. I encouraged them to tell me their feelings. It was very good for them to be able to express themselves and still be accepted, though it was painful to hear about their thoughts of suicide. I discovered a store-house of my own unresolved and unexpressed anger. I was over-whelmed at how much forgiveness had to be directed to myself, especially for not providing safety for my children in their own home. They will need to do recovery work about this for the rest of their lives.

My wounded spirit began to find healing through time spent in prayer and worship. I sensed that God wanted to heal me and restore me to wholeness. This was a whole new relation-ship with Jesus Christ. I had been imprisoned by church rules and legalism. I had never learned to be authentic. Now, as I turned to the comfort of old hymns, I discovered new words and melodies emerging from somewhere deep inside me. I dis-covered that I could write songs. I began opening my spirit to God in times of solitude, and privately sang these songs at my old black piano.

The songs expressed worship and dependence on "Jehovah-Jirah, God provider." When I wrote my songs, layers of hurt and anger began melting away. I praised God for my own uniqueness. As I quieted myself into hours of uninterrupted si-lence, Bible reading, prayer, and quiet listening, I began honestly searching for Jesus, and in doing this, I became more honest with myself. It was not easy to learn self-acceptance, but as I took the risk, I discovered a person inside me I had not known. This was not the person my parents expected her to be, or the person Al wanted that could never measure up. I began to be myself. Now I would be able to let others know me and know my pain. I also learned to trust myself in decisions and choices. For the first time in my life people weren't telling me what I should do. I could make my own choices, and I liked the ones I made.

Two friendships provided support during the divorce and the rebuilding process. These friendships helped me open up to a new dimension as I was gradually able to share my sorrow and needs. My friends had longed to care but had not known how, because I had been unable to share with them and let them see my despair. Now they were able to pray with me and to provide practical help by looking after the children. A friend outside the church recommended I explore Al-Anon and gave me information about other twelve-step groups. I began attending Al-Anon and Adult Children of Alcoholics meetings. The first few times I went, I just sat there and wept as I listened to these people who could be honest about themselves — people whose lives had been sabotaged by the same destruction as mine.

Journalling helped me to express the pent-up feelings and to recognize my own responsibility for past wounds. Books helped too. As my support network expanded, I enjoyed many friendships with women who had also suffered. Together we explored our lives and encouraged each other. I began leading weekly support group meetings for others like myself. I realized that the abuse I had experienced was greatly intertwined with church legalism and patriarchal structures. I was trained by a family system and by the church to stay in the marriage no matter what. I had not heard of women's shelters. I did not know about community support.

As I became freed from crippling emotional pain, I was able to explore new churches until I found one that accepted me. There, I met my second husband, to whom I have been married for the last four years. With him I have discovered that an intimate marital relationship is possible in a climate of nurture, affirmation, and mutual respect.

Chapter Four

Abuse and the Church

The gender roles assigned to women in society are reflected both in women's roles in marriage and in the way women perceive themselves. Western society has traditionally been patriarchal. In other words, its social structures and relationships are hierarchical, ranking males above females and those with greater power above those with less. Although these long-established patterns are changing, they still hold true to a large extent. In patriarchal societies, women have tended to see themselves as weak, submissive, and intended for the service of men. Wife abuse is one result. Women's tolerance of abuse is another.

The church is called to proclaim the good news of hope to the oppressed, but since it never lives entirely apart from the culture in which it finds itself, it has absorbed patriarchal assumptions and attitudes and has generated its own patriarchal structures. Consequently, in Christian societies, it has played a large part in establishing and maintaining the perception that women are weak and submissive, and that they are to be subject to men. This chapter considers how the church's language, culture, and thinking have contributed to abuse and women's tolerance of abuse. It also shows how the church in recent years has been waking up to the issues and transforming its own positions.

Throughout much of history, male violence toward women has been socially, legally, and religiously endorsed. The assumption that women were inferior and subservient to men was translated into practices that resulted in women being denied autonomous civil status. Even the images of literature and art have justified violence against women who transgressed custom or crossed men's wills. They were treated legally as permanent minors dependent upon fathers and husbands. In ancient Greece, wife and children were considered a man's property. In Roman law, women were considered to be the property of those on whom they were financially dependent (Ezell, 1998). The tradition that generated the Jewish scriptures, which Christians call the Old Testament, maintained that a wife was a chattel, a possession with which the husband could do as he pleased. With notable exceptions, women in ancient times were excluded from playing significant public roles and from involvement in the civic and religious life of the community.

This practice of the man controlling and managing his wife with absolute authority continued in European society and law after the establishment of Christianity as the state religion of the Roman Empire. During the Dark Ages and in the Middle Ages, women were subjugated, physically punished, and reminded of their inferior status in a world dominated by men. Both church and state gave husbands the legal right to beat their wives (General Synod Report, 1986; Martin, 1987). Fortune (1982) quotes a fifteenth-century publication called "Rules of Marriage" instructing men to scold and beat their wives.

With the considerable political, social, and religious change that came with the Renaissance and Reformation, women were still considered inferior beings who must submit to dominant husbands and serve them (Martin, 1987). Protestant leaders supported and encouraged physical discipline of women, as evidenced in the writings of Luther, Knox, and Calvin. According to Luther, women were created on an equal level with men, but because of the Fall, the story in the book of Genesis that pictures the woman, Eve, as tempted by the serpent, women must now be punished by God through subjugation to men; the husband is to rule and the wife is compelled to obey. Luther boasted of boxing his wife's ears, while Calvin commanded women to endure whatever treatment they received from their husbands out of duty to God.

There are even instances of women being subjected to savage punishments, such as special muzzles that held their mouths closed. These practices were sanctioned by a theology that described God as desiring a patriarchal order and taught that victims are sanctified through their suffering (Brown and Bohn, 1989). As late as the nineteenth century, married women were prevented from owning property, making contracts, or prosecuting husbands for beating them. In England, the writings of people such as John Stuart Mill and Mary Wollstoncraft began to challenge such beliefs, and gradually laws have been changed. However, the church has often been slow in keeping up with secular society in changing attitudes toward the role of women (General Synod Report, 1986)

Traditional attitudes toward women still linger and are reflected even now in the assumption that marriage and family are necessarily based on power. Contemporary sociological theory traces wife abuse to a societal power structure that elevates men to dominant positions and to the process that socializes both men and women into accepting the assumption of male dominance. Children learn gender identity in the family, and each family reflects the surrounding culture and the history of the culture. When families belong to a church, they absorb both secular and church culture. Often the church culture contains stronger traces of old assumptions of male dominance and female inferiority than the secular, or at least reinforces the secular attitudes.

Children are socialized to certain behaviours through a process whereby behaviours, thoughts, and attitudes are reinforced by reward and punishment. As they grow up, girls and boys are exposed to differing expectations. Girls observe other females who have assumed the role of submissive wife and mother, and they follow the models. Boys observe that maleness is demonstrated in aggression and power, and they too follow the models. Over the last two decades our society has seen many changes, as women have begun to infiltrate professions formerly dominated by men. However, there still remains a tendency to associate independence with men and passivity and dependence with women. Such a division encourages women to rely on men for protection and to submit to male authority — behaviours that set them up to tolerate abuse and even to feel responsible for it.

When scripture and church tradition are interpreted to suggest that women are inferior and subordinate to men, the effect in a Christian family may be to reinforce these attitudes. Consequently, some Christian women enter marriage with the expectation that they will serve their husband, obey him, and follow his lead in decision making. They connect with men conditioned in a similar way. It is not surprising that subsequent relationships are predisposed to exhibit some form of wife abuse.

Especially in conservative evangelical and conservative

catholic circles, certain key Christian concepts such as submission, headship, redemptive suffering, and forgiveness have been employed to perpetuate images of women as being less than their husbands. When these are combined with the expectation that marriage is forever, they contribute to a woman's position of powerlessness within marriage.

Submission

In Christian history, submission to the will of God has often been understood to include submission to earthly authority, since hierarchical structure has been seen as a means by which God's will is imposed. Therefore, submission and obedience have been regarded as moral virtues. In traditional hierarchical structures men take precedence over women. For example, the church's clerical leadership has until recently been entirely male; in fact, the women whose stories appear in this book turned for help to pastors, all of whom were male. Like the church, the family is an extension of the greater social and political hierarchy.

Not surprisingly, encouraging women to defer to their husbands in decision making and spiritual matters has helped to foster wife abuse. It has been taught that the woman must submit to her husband no matter how the man behaves, and that her loving submission will win the husband to the Lord, though the cost may be violence to herself.

Headship

In traditional imagery, the church is the bride of Christ, and Christ is the head of the church. In marriage, the husband is to the wife what Christ is to the church: the loving head to whom she must submit. Women are thus encouraged to listen to their husbands, honour them, and follow their direction. One implication of headship is that the key to a happy marriage lies in the wife's willingness to accept a dependent role. Within this framework, events and decisions revolve around the wife's ability to meet her husband's needs, because he is her leader.

Redemptive suffering

Some Christian women believe that suffering within a marriage is God's will; therefore, through suffering there will be learning and redemption. This notion is rooted in the belief that redemption has been made available to us through the suffering and death of Jesus Christ. From this perspective all suffering is redemptive because it is connected to Christ's suffering. Women may apply this understanding to the suffering of a mistreated wife and be convinced that her suffering may redeem a confused husband. Since suffering is seen as a moral virtue to be embraced, wives derive a measure of comfort from believing that God will teach them and purify them through their plight. Such a position perpetuates a denial of reality and motivates a woman to ignore her own needs for a nurturing relationship, in order to be faithful to her husband and to God.

Forgiveness

The forgiveness extended to us by a loving God is to be emulated as we forgive those who have hurt us. To offer forgiveness is to give up the right to hold the injustice against the one who has wronged us. Forgiveness offers freedom and health when applied with godly wisdom. Unfortunately it has also been used to mislead women to endure abuse, exhorting them to forgive the abuser and grant him another chance, instead of encouraging them to forgive the abuse and get help for themselves or move out of the situation. Whipple (1987) describes situations where women were led to be more tolerant and understanding and to forgive the beatings just as Christ has forgiven them. They were advised to believe that God would miraculously intervene and change their husbands.

Destructive pastoral attitudes

As recently as the 1980s, studies revealed that many clergy still believe that God had ordained patriarchal structures. In the early twenty-first century, vestiges of this belief may remain, even in those mainline churches where a great shift in attitude has taken place. As we have seen, these patriarchal structures support the abuse of women (Barnett and LaViolette, 1993).

Some American studies, conducted among women with conservative evangelical affiliations, revealed some startling attitudes. Women who sought help from their pastors were told that, if they left their husbands, "you have an unforgiving spirit and a root of bitterness" (Johnson and VanVonderen, 1991). You should "stay and work things out," and "try harder not to provoke him" (Horton, Wilkins, and Wright, 1988). Many pastors expressed a desire to preserve the marriage at any cost to the women. A study by Alsdurf and Alsdurf (1989) revealed that 92 per cent of interviewed pastors declared that they would never tell a woman to divorce her abuser. Most pastors were more willing to accept a marriage in which some abuse occurred than to counsel a woman to separate. Many respondents expressed concern that the husband's violence not be overemphasized or used to justify breaking the marriage commitment.

Traditional language

The church's traditional language has spoken of God as male, using the masculine pronouns "he" and "him" (often capitalized) to refer to God. There has often been marked opposition to attempts to change Bible translations, liturgies, and hymns to inclusive language. Even in speaking of the human race, it has proven difficult for the church to change familiar passages so that "my brothers" can become "my brothers and sisters" or "all men" can become "all people." Significantly, all the abused wives whose stories appear in this book refer to God as "he." Even Lily, who found herself unable to continue applying the image of father to God, opted to address her prayers to Jesus, conceived as a friend, rather than to God conceived as mother. This linguistic patriarchalism has undoubtedly contributed to women's sense of being second best, although new liturgies, hymns, and Bible translations are increasingly sensitive to the problem.

Old attitudes outlive official changes

There can be no doubt that the church's emphasis on the permanence of marriage has caused many women over the ages to remain in abusive marriages. During the Middle Ages, marriage law fell into the church's province and was maintained with the legal authority of secular power. In the twentieth century, as the influence of the church has waned, the state has taken an increasingly liberal attitude toward the permanence of marriage, making separation and divorce ever easier. The church has sought to maintain the standards of Christian marriage, but the churches and people within the churches are at different stages in their attitudes toward the permanence of marriage and the abuse within marriage. One example will have to suffice.

As long ago as 1967, the Anglican Church of Canada made provision for remarriage of divorced persons in church. Behind this decision lay the recognition that some divorces at least are admissable — in other words, that not all marriages are forever. Canon XXI, the church's law on marriage, says, "In the New Testament a new standard of reciprocal love between husband and wife was introduced leading toward an understanding of their equality…. In Christ's name separated spouses were encouraged to seek reconciliation. In his name also divorce was forbidden, though not without exception" (Handbook of General Synod, 2002).

The Anglican Church, like other churches, distinguishes between separation and divorce, which occur when a marriage has broken down, and annulment, which may be granted if certain conditions required for a valid marriage were not present or were ignored at the time the marriage took place. "Consent to marry is not present where one of the parties at the time of the covenant of marriage was deceived … with respect to violence, sadistic conduct, or other abnormal practices." Such a marriage might well qualify for annulment.

Divorces granted by secular authority, even for reasons other than the defects listed in the marriage canon, may also be recognized by the church, subject to certain provisions, including safeguards for former spouses and the children of former marriages. They also include "efforts having been made in good faith before the dissolution [of the marriage] to effect reconciliation.…"

Moreover, if the official marriage commission hearing the application for remarriage is satisfied "that efforts toward reconciliation … would have been ineffective," the commission may still recognize the divorce and permit remarriage in church (quotations from Canon XXI).

Yet, in spite of all this, Dr. Anne Tanner (1990) notes that, although the church now makes provision for the remarriage of divorced persons, it has no official way of recognizing that a marriage has failed. It "still has no official pastoral guidelines for those going through separation and divorce, nor is there any formal indication that the institutional church has any pastoral responsibility for them unless they wish to remarry in church" (p. 48). Also, speaking personally, she says what many women feel who are considering or have been through separation: "It was my own internal experience of being 'outside' … which now separated me from … a church which upheld married couples and lifelong marriage as the norm and made little provision for marriages that did not work" (p. 9).

Rereading the scriptures

It is no longer possible to ignore the fact that the books of the Bible reflect attitudes and assumptions of cultures in which they were composed, and that when we read them now, we bring to them attitudes and assumptions of our own culture. The Bible was written by fallible human beings, but Christians also believe that it contains the Word of God. The challenge is to discern the Word of God in the Bible.

Smedes (1983) suggests that the seventh commandment, "you shall not commit adultery" (Exodus 20:14), refers to any violation of the marital relationship. From this perspective, abuse is a form of adultery. If it takes place, the marriage covenant has been broken and the abused partner is free to leave.

We have already noted that, in the patriarchal society of the Old Testament, women took an inferior role. Wives were owned by their husbands, and their principal role was to produce sons to continue the male line of tribal or clan inheritance. Only husbands had the power to initiate divorce. When, therefore, the prophet Malachi has God say, "I hate divorce" (see Malachi 2:14–16), he is declaring a principle that is intended to protect women from being cast off without good reason in a society where, as divorced ex-wives, they would have no status or economic livelihood at all. Malachi berates men for being faithless to their wives. God, he says, hates divorce because of the pain it causes, and furthermore God hates anyone "covering one's garment with violence" in marriage.

Jesus seems to have had similar concerns in mind when he says: "It was also said, 'Whoever divorces his wife, let him give her a certificate of divorce.' But I say to you that anyone who divorces his wife, except on the ground of unchastity, causes her to commit adultery; and whoever marries a divorced woman commits adultery" (Matthew 5:31–2). Here Jesus is introducing a whole new principle: the idea that a man could commit adultery. Up to this point, the term "adultery" had been applied only to women's sexual activity outside marriage (Tanner, 1990, p. 32). This is further evidence of Jesus' intention of protecting women from being abused by men.

St. Paul's letters were written at a time when he and other Christians expected the immediate second coming of Christ. He wanted people to prepare for this great event, not to be distracted by sex and marriage, and consequently he strongly advocated celibacy. But realizing the impossibility of imposing this discipline on the entire Christian community, he made provision for marriage in terms that make it seem little more than a licensed outlet for sexual desire. He also makes detailed provisions, including the possibility of divorce, for marriages between believers and unbelievers (1 Corinthians 7:1–16). His rule that neither partner should leave the other has to be understood in this first-century context. He is careful, however, to lay the rule on both men and women. Like Jesus, Paul is protecting women from being simply cast off or abused.

Citing Ephesians 5:21–33, which directs both the man and the woman to "be subject to one another out of reverence for Christ," Martin (1987) discusses the implications of reciprocity and accountability implicit in the command to submit. Thus, mutual submission becomes the model for relationships of mutual respect and kindness. In our own day we can recognize, in Jesus' and Paul's insistence that both man and woman share the responsibility for making the marriage work, the foundation for our understanding that men and women are equals in the marriage.

St. Paul says that neither partner should separate from the other, as if divorce is itself a form of abuse. However, if a Christian marries an unbeliever and the unbeliever breaks off the relationship, then, says St. Paul, "Let it be so. In such a case, the brother or sister [*i.e.*, the Christian] is not bound [*i.e.*, to the marriage]" and is free to remarry. Whipple (1987) argues that breaking the relationship, for example by violence or abuse, is an act of faithlessness that puts the offending partner into the position of an unbeliever who breaks the relationship and leaves the other partner free of the relationship if she chooses to be. Fortune (1987) argues that, when violence occurs in a marriage, it is a form of unfaithfulness because it destroys trust. God grieves the unfaithfulness that results in divorce, but it is the unfaithfulness that breaks the marriage covenant.

Teachings regarding forgiveness have contributed to learned helplessness, by leading women to believe that they can do nothing to end the abuse except to pray (Kauffman-Kennel, 1987). But the New Testament message is one of liberation and freedom from oppression. When the abuser has already violated the covenant and destroyed family unity by using violence, forgiveness does not require the abused wife to remain in the situation. The appropriate role of forgiveness is to set the abused person free by allowing her to relinquish her resentment.

A Christian Reformed Church study on physical, emotional, and sexual abuse (1992) insists that abuse is a sin and a violation of the marriage commitment. A similar report published by the Anglican Church (General Synod Report, 1986) suggests that the church needs to recognize violence as abhorrent to the Christian understanding of family and home. The Mennonite Central Committee (1991) declares that the church has great potential as a vital resource to families who are experiencing domestic violence; pastors and lay members can more fully realize this potential when they are better informed about the issue.

Deeply entrenched views of marriage and the role of women have, in the past, influenced the church to preach that the sanctity of marriage takes precedence over the life of the individual. But attitudes are changing fast, and so is the church's teaching. Women, such as those whose stories appear in this book, are being set free from fear. The Anglican marriage canon says that all members of the church share the responsibility for "uphold[ing] Christian standards of marriage in human society" (General Synod Handbook, 2002). Today we have to understand that this responsibility includes assisting those whose marriages are abusive and those whose marriages come to an end. This book is intended to help church members take up that responsibility.

Chapter Five

Marie

"I lived in constant fear."

From the time I was small I knew that God was always present everywhere. Religion was still taught in the schools, and I learned strict religious values and rules. At the age of seven or eight I made a conscious decision to believe in God.

My mother was divorced. She had three children by her first husband, and when they parted, her husband took the children and prevented her from ever seeing them again. I was the only child of my mother's second marriage, and when I was born, my mother held on tightly to me. She was overpowering in her efforts to keep me from harm. Even as a young child, I felt that she intruded on me. She was going to make me perfect. She tried to control everything I did, and since she didn't accept me as a separate person, I retreated inside myself to hide from her and protect the sensitive part of me. I can now understand that losing her three other children was the reason for her suffocating behaviour.

When I was seventeen I met my first husband. Having lived such a sheltered life, I was very naive. Looking back, I see that he showed all the signs of an abuser. He'd show up late for dates and keep me waiting for up to two hours, but he always had a good excuse. I was so madly in love that nothing made any difference. I believe I sensed God telling me not to marry Tom, but I ignored the warning, and after we married I turned away from my religious values and focused on meeting Tom's needs.

Tom, a heavy drinker, began abusing me immediately after the wedding. He had drastic mood swings: when he was nice, he was very, very nice; but when he wasn't, he was horrid. He put me down constantly. He told me I was ugly and stupid, and if he heard me singing, he would say, "You know you can't sing. Why do you make that noise?" I adapted my behaviour to cope with the abuse, increased my attempts to make him happy, and tried to avoid doing the things that made him angry.

Soon he started being violent. He pushed me around, shoved me into furniture, hit me hard, and sometimes bruised my face. Sometimes he'd throw things at me. We did not talk a lot because he was the breadwinner, the man who went out and made a living, and I was just the wife who looked after the home. He spent most of what he made on himself, and I saw very little of the money. Since I soon became pregnant, I did not work.

After my first child was born, I lived in poverty because Tom gave us no money. On one occasion, the baby and I went without enough food for a week. My parents brought me food because they knew something must be wrong, but we did not talk about it. That was the way things were in my family; we did not talk about problems. I had no friends because Tom discouraged me from talking to neighbours and got very angry if he thought someone had dropped in to visit. I started turning to God, as he was the only one I could talk to. I needed him to sustain me, as the physical violence increased and I suffered broken bones. I believed that I just had to put up with the abuse because there was no alternative: the Bible said that marriage is forever and that divorce cannot be considered. I knew what had happened to my mother, and I thought that God was punishing her because God hates divorce.

As the abuse got worse I became a zombie, trying to cope with the episodes of violence by withdrawing into myself. After one beating, when Tom hit me in the side of the head, I suffered an ear problem. When I went to the doctor, he said the problem was nerves and gave me Valium. He must have known or suspected that I was being abused and thought that Valium would help me cope, but he said nothing about the relationship. I have had a chronic ear problem since and am now deaf in that ear.

I wanted to stay in the relationship because of the good periods. Each time after Tom hit me, he was very sorry, and I felt sorry for him because he was so troubled. I'd tell myself it was right to stay in the marriage. During the next two years I had another child. The abuse continued and I was isolated from everyone except my parents, but I told them nothing of the abuse, and they never asked.

I believe that prayer and my relationship with God were the only things that kept me alive. I felt as if I was not even a person, just someone who had to survive from hour to hour, living in terror of Tom. I kept calling out to God to keep me going. I did not go to church because Tom became angry at any mention of religion. I had a good grounding in scripture from my school years. I was taught to sing the Lord's Prayer. Often I sat with my hands over my ears and sang the Lord's Prayer or the Twenty-third Psalm. I'd let the words soak in, giving comfort. I kept the children out of Tom's way by putting them to bed early. They were afraid of him.

Eventually, I confided in my parents, and on two occasions

I left Tom for a couple of days and went to stay with them. They, however, were meek timid people who were terrified of Tom, and they encouraged me to go back so that he would not hurt me, the children, or them. In each case, when I returned, Tom beat me up severely. Once he was so scared that I would leave for good that he came to my parents' house and pounded on the door, making all kinds of threats.

Somewhere in the turmoil I began to pray blessings on Tom. The result was a change in me. I started to be more objective and to see what his violence was doing. Then one day when Tom came home, the children ran and hid under the couch, and he was so angry that he tried to strangle me. At that point I called out to God and I heard God's voice. It told me to leave. Soon after that, my parents came and picked me up and took me to a motel, where I stayed with the children for two or three weeks. I did not know where else to go or what help I could get, but my mother found out that I could apply for welfare.

I talked to a social worker, and that was the first time I had told anyone other than my parents about the abuse. Back then you did not talk about violence in marriage because it did not happen to decent people. I felt that the marriage problems were all my fault and that I should go back to the marriage, but when the social worker talked to me about family violence, I was relieved just to know that it was recognized and taken seriously. Before long I filed for divorce and went through the motions in a dazed way. I believe that it was my relationship with God that led me out of the marriage.

After I left, I joined a church congregation where I participated in Bible studies and prayer meetings. I was happy that I was finally free to go to church. It was still a struggle to be single and cope with the children, but I was free. It was also a luxury to have money for groceries and the freedom to control a small budget. I started to gain a fragile sense of myself as a real person, not just someone who went through the motions of surviving from day to day.

Unfortunately, I failed to receive any counselling to help me understand what had happened in the marriage, and very little healing took place. It was not long before I met a man named Chuck, who promised to take care of me and the children. A woman from the church warned me to stay away from him as she could see he was not good for me, and she felt God telling her to warn me. I dismissed her as a crazy prophet type, and within a year of my divorce I married Chuck. I even gave up church involvement because he did not like it, and soon I slipped right back into denying who I was again and became the submissive little wife, moulding myself to what he required.

As soon as we were married Chuck became more controlling and verbally aggressive. He forbade me to have friends and to work, so I stayed home alone with the children and tried to please him. He gave me very little from his high earnings; once again I had to scrape pennies together for food. At least he was not violent. Nevertheless, I once more became completely isolated, talking to no one, not even my parents. Chuck was often away from the house for long periods, working, drinking, or pursuing his many hobbies, but he never relaxed his control. Even if I went to the store for bread, he would phone me when I was due to get back. I lived in fear, doing what he told me. To me this seemed normal.

For over ten years I endured the abuse. The children were becoming rude to me all the time and wouldn't do anything I asked them to do. I could not understand this change because we had been very close during the years of my marriage to Tom. I could not see that my being such a zombie had an impact on them. I thought that I loved them, took care of them, and did all the things a mum should do. I had no idea how deprived they were of a mother's deep genuine love and nurture. A huge turning point for me was when my younger daughter told me that Chuck had made sexual advances to her. I was paralysed with fear: fear for her if he found out that I knew, fear for myself, and fear for the future. It made me start to see the awfulness of the marriage, but I could not leave because I felt so weak, and I could not tell Chuck because of my fear.

I kept praying to God for understanding. Finally, I joined a church, but fearing Chuck's response, I kept it from him. It was like coming home. From that point my life began to change. I got involved in some of the activities and made acquaintances. As I observed their marriages, I became even more aware of how terrible my situation was.

Eventually the children both ran away from home. I was devastated when they told me they could no longer live with Chuck because of his anger, his abuse, and his attitude to me. My younger daughter could not understand my inability to do anything to help either her or myself. That was another turning point. I went to a pastor and asked him to help me make sense of things, but he was of the fundamentalist belief that marriage is sacred and should come before even my children's welfare. So I hung on and stayed with Chuck. This almost destroyed the children and my relationship with them.

Finally I tried to leave and went to an apartment for a short time. The church community was a place where I could see myself as a person of worth and where my children could visit without fear. But then Chuck began attending the church. People liked him and asked why I would leave such a nice man. They told me that God hates divorce and I would be committing a dreadful sin. I stopped working with my counsellor and made the terrible mistake of going back for another four years.

This was devastating for the children. Being older by then, they refused to come back home.

One Sunday I met a church member who invited me to volunteer at a women's shelter, and I knew God was telling me to go there. Suddenly I could see what had happened to me. When I got home, I cried for five hours. It was such a relief to know that I was not the only person on the planet who was going through all this. It felt like God was there with me, saying it was okay. God showed me that I was important to him and that I should never have been treated like that. I realized that Chuck and I did not have a marriage at all. We did not talk to each other and I knew nothing about him, and even less about our finances.

A little voice inside had always told me it was wrong to stay in the marriage. I knew God's voice well, because I had listened to him in my darkest moments when there was nothing else to hear. Gradually I grew stronger. A counsellor helped me see that my life and my children's lives were very valuable and I should not sacrifice them for the marriage. I began learning to care about myself and to risk letting people get to know me a little. Finally the day came when I made the decision to leave the marriage. I had gone to a church function and when I left, instead of going home, I went to my mother's. I thought, "I am a child of God and I do not have to live like this. This is ridiculous."

The next day, while Chuck was at work, I went back to the house, collected my things, and went to live with my parents. My children were living with friends. Chuck made many attempts to reconcile the situation, but God kept telling me not to go back.

I had heard so much church teaching on the permanence of marriage; that is why I had stayed so long. But I heard the voice that I knew well, and it kept telling me I should keep away. I felt guilt and shame whenever I went to church, but I knew that Chuck also belonged to God.

Soon I started attending a different church, where I made lots of new friends. I joined a women's Bible study group and became involved with a group of women who met together for prayer and fellowship. For a time I worked at a retreat centre and lived in the caring and supportive community there, feeling that I belonged and was accepted for who I was. I did not have to perform to earn their love. This was a totally new experience that became a stepping-stone to a new job, and a place of my own. I got involved with dance and attended dance workshops. I also participated in some women's workshops, which helped improve my self-esteem. There I met other women who had suffered, and some who were still in the place that I had been. These were healing experiences.

Seven years after the divorce, I am getting on with my life. I attend a church where I feel accepted. I still have a lot of guilt and sadness regarding my children. They will take many years to heal from their wounds, and it will take me many years to heal from the guilt and knowledge of the pain that I caused them. But I have many friends, and I am doing things I enjoy, and no one tells me when to go out and when to come home. I have a very close relationship with the God who loves me. I am now free.

Chapter Six

The Seven S's of Staying

The women whose stories appear in this book decided initially to stay in their marriages, and an analysis of their stories shows that they had reasons in common for doing so. They were influenced by a complex array of beliefs about themselves and their relationships, life experiences, religion, and marriage. Their decisions to endure arose out of the interactive effect of all these factors, which are summarized below under seven headings.

1. System problems

During our lives we interact with many systems. The first and most powerful is the family of origin. It influences the way we think and feel about ourselves, others, and the world around us. We absorb our parents' beliefs about what is good or bad, what is important or unimportant, what is to be valued and what is not. These beliefs combine with childhood experiences and influence an individual's adult attitudes and behaviours. Four sub-themes emerged in the women's stories of their formative years: boundary issues, conflict with parents, generational problems, and rigid family rules.

Boundary issues (see Appendix A, p. 131)

Families possess both external and internal boundaries. The external boundary separates the family from other families and outside influences, whereas the internal boundary operates between people within the family. Boundaries need to be flexible, allowing certain information and experiences to enter while keeping other influences out. Sometimes, however, boundaries can be either too rigid or too weak. In the families of the women studied, boundaries were rarely flexible: most were too rigid, but some were too weak.

When families of the women in the study had rigid external boundaries, family members were isolated and unable to experience friendships. Women and children were often prevented from developing warm trusting relationships outside the family. When families experienced weak external boundaries, they allowed almost anyone to enter the family space. In such cases, children were unprotected from the exterior environment and prevented from feeling part of a family unit.

Rigid internal boundaries acted as walls that isolated individuals from others in the family. They experienced a lack of communication and intimacy and felt misunderstood, abandoned, and unable to experience a sense of themselves as worthwhile individuals. Rigid internal boundaries between generations resulted in little authentic communication between adults and children. People performed their roles in the family but experienced little closeness or trust.

Weak internal boundaries between family members inhibited

the development of a strong sense of self as unique and special. In such cases parents would tell the child how to think, feel, and act, leaving little opportunity for the child to learn about herself and her world. This led to one or both parents being overinvolved with the children and "smothering" them. Weak internal boundaries between generations often led to role-reversal, with children being expected to provide adult care to parents. In some cases, a lack of generational boundaries resulted in incestuous relationships.

Difficulties with boundaries inhibited each woman's ability to develop a strong sense of herself as an individual, and impeded her ability to decide what she should or should not tolerate from other people.

Conflictual or distant relationships with parents

All the women experienced their fathers as distant and controlling. Fathers were not available to talk or discuss issues: they held rigid attitudes and enforced strict rules. Distant mothers were often described as passive, aloof, and unsupportive. Daughters perceived these mothers to be intensely involved with their husbands and not available to nurture and comfort their children.

Conflict between children and parents prompted either harsh outbursts of anger or long periods of silence. Some of the women were subjected to extreme physical punishment while others experienced emotional abuse in the form of put-downs, constant criticism, and ridicule.

Parents provided limited nurturing for these women during childhood. As adults, the women experienced an inability to identify healthy or unhealthy behaviours in their own marital relationships and tended to tolerate behaviour that was demeaning. As difficulties escalated in the marriage, they were reluctant to reach out to the family of origin for help, for fear of being criticized and ridiculed.

Dysfunctional generational patterns

Controlling fathers and compliant mothers often replicated the patterns of previous generations. The women recreated these patterns in their marriages by being compliant and self-effacing. Many families reflected generations of parents who were unable to meet the emotional needs of their children. With childhood needs unmet, women were ill equipped to nurture themselves or their own children.

Rigid family rules and roles

Many of the women married to escape their family's strict roles and rules. Most had experienced a strict religious upbringing. Children were expected to make a good impression on others and adhere to certain standards of conduct. Slotted into roles within the family, they experienced emotional distance and a lack of authenticity on the part of their parents, who communicated lack of permission to be authentic. Because small children in such families are not allowed to verbalize their pain, they internalized and suppressed it. Many of the women commented that they inadvertently assumed a role within the family and related to the rest of the family out of that role (see Appendix B, p. 135).

2. Sense of self

A strong sense of self develops when a child has been nurtured, affirmed, and allowed to explore different behaviours and attitudes. When this freedom is lacking, a child grows up with a somewhat fragile sense of who she is and a pervasive feeling of being incomplete. Most of the women recalled that, at the time they first encountered their respective mates, they possessed no clear idea of themselves apart from belonging to family and church.

Married at a young age with little appreciation of self

All the women had married before age twenty, although Marie's second marriage occurred when she was a little older. Most had met and begun dating their future husbands while in their mid-teens. They either had gone directly from their families into the marriage, or from family to Christian boarding school to marriage, exchanging one controlling situation for another. Therefore, they had enjoyed little opportunity for self-discovery and failed to achieve the emotional separation from family that occurs when an individual realizes she is a person with her own identity.

Being defined by others

The childhood and teen years offered limited opportunity for discussion of options and alternative approaches to situations. There was little parental tolerance for behaviours that deviated from family norms. As a result, the women became the people their families wanted them to be. Marriage recreated a similar situation: the husband maintained control over his wife, expecting and often demanding that she fulfil certain roles.

The women experienced little personal growth in childhood or marriage. They depended on husbands for a sense of well-being as the marriages afforded little opportunity for experimentation or self-development.

Weak boundaries around the self

Engel (1990) asserts, "We all need to have a private psychological space that belongs to us and to us alone." An emotional boundary provides that space, defines who we are, and gives us the power to control who has input into our lives. It also determines what behaviours we will tolerate from others and ourselves. The women experienced weak emotional boundaries that left them vulnerable to the ideas and beliefs of others, especially their partners. They were unable to put limits on their own behaviour or on that of others.

3. Shame

According to John Bradshaw (1988), shame is a normal human emotion that keeps us within our boundaries by letting us know that we can and will make mistakes. Shame is the psychological foundation of humility. This healthy emotion, however, can be transformed into a destructive force that takes over a person's whole identity. Bradshaw suggests that "to have shame as an identity is to believe that one's being is flawed, that one is defective as a human being."

Thus, an individual experiences shame when, at the core of

her being, she does not believe that she is lovable. The women's experiences of shame had roots in their early years. In relationships with family, community, and church, the women felt inadequate and unlovable. They felt judged and condemned by those around them. Within their marriages they felt inferior. As the abuse increased, fear of rejection, humiliation, and condemnation prevented the women from confiding in others for help. Shame kept them bound. They avoided reaching out to others, became isolated, and felt apprehensive about disclosing the abuse.

Limited acceptance

When parents base acceptance of children on performance, the children fail to derive a sense of worth and confidence, becoming susceptible to feelings of shame. A lack of acceptance equates with abandonment and results in the loss of one's authentic self. All the women experienced a lack of acceptance, and believed that, if other people really knew them, they would not be loved. To hide their feelings of unworthiness, they wore "good Christian masks." Unable to present honest images to others, they deprived themselves of the opportunity to experience genuine acceptance. They were unable to disclose the events that stabbed at the core of their beings and their marriages — the abuse.

Superficial relationships

When a person is unable to trust others, relationships will lack emotional honesty. Individuals will be unable to disclose their deep concerns, needs, fears, and ideas, or to hear those of others. The women had experienced limited emotional honesty in relationships and believed that others would not accept them if they revealed their true selves They related to others in ways they believed were expected, without going beyond the surface of their lives. Thus they were deprived of the opportunity to be known and really to know others. As a result, vulnerability to the husband's ideas and beliefs increased in such a way as to leave them dependent and isolated.

4. Stress of the abuse

Feelings of helplessness, numbness, and confusion reflected the impact of married lives that lacked nurture and affirmation, and instead provided humiliation in a variety of forms.

Constant criticism and ridicule

Having received criticism in childhood, the women believed they were defective. This rendered them vulnerable to their husbands' degrading comments. With greater exposure to derogatory statements, they became further weakened in confidence and self-esteem.

Isolation

In spite of church involvement, the women felt isolated and alone. Unable to share thoughts and feelings with others, they found even superficial interaction to be an effort. This distance prevented them from obtaining honest feedback from others, or from being able to check out the reality of their perceptions. The only source of "reality" then became the husband's criticisms.

Often, husbands limited their wives' contact with others, thus depriving them of the opportunity to observe the interactions of other couples. The resulting dependency left them with no other gauge of reality than their husbands' definitions of them as wives, mothers, and women.

Post-traumatic stress disorder

Symptoms resembling those of post-traumatic disorder (see Appendix C, p. 140) were evident in the women's stories of their responses to abuse. They experienced numbness, flashbacks, hyper-vigilance, and a heightened startle reflex, along with feelings of severe fatigue, nausea, aching muscles, and dizziness. Hyper-vigilance manifested as a constant awareness of what was happening in the environment, while a heightened startle reflex was reported as a tendency to "jump" upon hearing sharp sounds. Exhaustion and weakness immobilized the women and thwarted their ability to generate alternative coping strategies. They experienced nightmares and became sleep deprived. Unable to think clearly, they could not unravel the conflict and confusion in the relationship. They became attentive to their husbands verbal and non-verbal cues, trying to keep control yet having little. Such efforts produced exhaustion and fatigue, which resulted in the women tolerating the abuse for many years, even after they recognized its severity.

Fear of change

Although the women feared their husbands, their depleted emotional resources and lack of confidence inspired a fear of any type of change. Some were terrified that they might fall apart if they made any changes in relationships or living arrangements.

Defence mechanisms

Defence mechanisms (see Appendix D, p. 143) occur when people are afraid of becoming overwhelmed by experiences and develop ways of blocking reality from their minds by distorting their perceptions through denial, minimization, rationalization, and delusion.

Denial causes a person to refuse to acknowledge a problem or recognize the extent of that problem. For the women, as tolerance of the abuse increased, so did denial. They protected themselves by refusing to acknowledge the problems, often for many years.

A partner of denial is *minimization*, which involves minimizing the seriousness of a situation to make it more acceptable. The women told themselves "things were not that bad" or that "other people get it far worse."

Rationalization is the process of creating reasons to explain why something is happening. The women kept the horror from their minds by rationalizing, "This is the way marriage is supposed to be," or "All men act this way; it's not just my husband." Other forms of rationalization involved the belief that "I must have deserved this," or "If I were a better wife, this would not happen."

Delusion blocks reality from one's mind by providing false beliefs that make a situation more palatable. Some of the women believed such delusions as, "My man is not the type of man who would hurt me badly."

Other coping strategies include suppression and repression. When *suppression* is employed, the individual consciously chooses to forget a trauma in order to block out the pain. The women fought to block the painful memories from consciousness.

Repression occurs when an individual is unaware of blocking out memories. Painful incidents were often recalled by the women following the divorce. They expressed surprise at not remembering these situations while still in the marriage.

Defence mechanisms prevented the women from comprehending the full reality of the abusive situation. These mechanisms helped the women adapt to abuse that most of us would not tolerate. They also contributed to the women's decisions to endure their marriages for many years, even when dangerous to do so.

5. Submission and relationship dynamics

Submission defined the women's roles in their marriages and caused them to be deferential, resulting in a tendency to succumb to the Cycle of Violence (Appendix E, p. 146). Relationship dynamics saw wives as dependent on their husbands for approval and guidance, yet feeling responsible for the health of the marriage.

Emotional dependency on husband

Husbands were the source of all nurturing and support, regardless of the infrequency with which these were provided. Each woman felt she would "die" without her spouse and became determined to "do anything" to gain her man's love. However, each experienced little closeness and most felt alone and abandoned. Often the emotional connection was fraught with conflict, but for women who felt cut off from others, even the conflict provided some relief from isolation. As emotional distance and conflict increased, the women experienced an even greater need for positive responses from their husbands.

Husband's control of decisions and finances

The women expected their husbands to make all decisions regarding family activities. When the women did make decisions and choices, these sparked sarcasm or ridicule. Thus, they lost confidence in their ability to make wise choices, believing that when husbands made decisions, wives were to "obey." Financial dependence on the husband, both real and imagined, kept the women believing that they had no alternative but to endure the abuse, despite the fact that several of them had demonstrated an ability to manage finances and obtain employment.

Pitying the husband

The women felt sorry for their husbands. They believed that their men had problems that stemmed from childhood wounding. Thinking that husbands need "more love and understanding," they expected destructive behaviours. Their concern was misinterpreted as "God's compassion," and motivated them to try harder to improve the marriages.

Feeling responsible for husband

The men expected their wives to rescue them from difficult situations, and their wives readily responded. Some wives made excuses for their men, while others secured employment to pay off debts from careless spending. The women felt responsible for running the household, caring for children, and contributing to the family income. They believed that somehow they had caused the abuse and were responsible for creating greater harmony in the home.

They felt a responsibility to change their husbands, and implored God to make them more dutiful wives. Some women were afraid that leaving would cause their husbands to "fall apart," and believed they could not do something that would have such a devastating effect.

Hope that the husband would change

The women clung to the hope that soon God would "perform a miracle" to change their husbands. Magical thinking motivated them to strive to be more loving wives so that husbands would respond to their care. They believed some change in their own behaviour, or the intervention of God, would effect a change in their husbands. They invested long hours in prayer, believing they could change their husbands into more loving partners by praying for healing for these angry men.

Fear of reprisals from husband

For some women, the fear of revenge by their husbands kept them bound. Upon leaving, some of them did experience harassment and assault.

The Cycle of Violence (see Appendix E, p. 146)

The Cycle of Violence involves three phases: tension building, escalation of tension, and contrition. This cycle is experienced both in cases where physical abuse dominates a relationship and in situations where emotional abuse occurs without physical violence. The women experienced angry outbursts of physical and emotional violence from their husbands, interspersed with periods of remorse and contrition. The positive reinforcement of remorse fuelled a hope that the husband might indeed change and strengthened the resolve to try again. Therefore, the cycle would recommence again. Tension built, the outburst occurred, and remorse followed.

With time, the angry tirades occurred more often and with increasing intensity, while periods of remorse grew fewer and less intense. This cycle was reinforced by prayer, because each period of remorse was seen as a sign that God was working and would restore the marriage. With constant repetition of the cycle, the women experienced an increasing dependency on their husbands. Their need for the positive reinforcement of contrition became heightened, and they found it more difficult to let go of the desire to make the marriage work. Therefore, each recurrence fuelled the desire to submit to these men, for whom a miracle might occur.

6. Scriptural interpretation

Churches influenced the women's willingness to stay in the relationship because they perpetuated gender-role stereotypes and the idea that marriage is forever. The influence of the church was a significant factor in decision making. Also, the hierarchy of the church gave men authority over women and the pastor authority over his congregation. These values were derived from the way scripture had been interpreted and presented.

Teaching that marriage is forever

The women believed that marriage is an institution that should last "until death." They had heard numerous statements to the effect that "God hates divorce." As a result, they believed that there was no excuse for divorce and that they were to submit to their husbands, in spite of mistreatment. Some women expressed a fear that they would anger God if they were to leave the marriage. They kept hoping that God would change their husbands.

Teaching regarding headship and submission

Church teaching relayed the message that men were to be heads over their wives, and that wives were to submit to male authority. Interpretation of these concepts created an expectation that husbands had the authority to control their homes, and wives must remain obedient despite abuse (see also chapter 4).

The hierarchy: Pastors have authority

Scriptural passages regarding the authority of the pastor led the women to believe that, in matters of divorce, pastors held the authority to tell them what to do. If pastors sanctioned certain actions, then these were considered permissible. Several women were encouraged by pastors to try harder, pray more, and make their marriages work.

Fear of being judged by the church

Although the scriptures abound with exhortations to love and not judge, passages regarding sin gave rise to a fear of judgement and condemnation. The women had heard others being judged and feared that they would receive condemnation should they separate from their husbands.

7. Societal expectations

Through modelling and interacting with society, the women acquired stereotypical values, expectations, and ideas about gender-roles. They believed that girls were to grow up and find a man to marry. Parents told daughters that they were praying for the right husband to come along, creating the idea that girls must get married. The women entered marriage with the expectation that they would raise children and care for men who would work to support them. The adoption of these gender roles kept the women tolerating situations involving abuse. Such conditioning created, in most of the women, a desire to serve their husbands, help them change, and save their marriages.

Chapter Seven

Barbara

*"I can't keep loving him
when I'm getting beat all the time."*

I grew up the second oldest of four children in a small rural community where everyone knew everyone else and church activities were an important part of community life. I was known in the town as a "good Christian girl," and people kind of put me on a pedestal. I felt a pressure all through my childhood to be a good girl and do as I was told. In school I did well until the age of nine. That's when I was raped.

Although I didn't tell anyone for over thirty years, it affected me. I couldn't concentrate in school. I had no self-confidence, and I became very withdrawn, but I still behaved like the good girl that I was supposed to be. I was ten years old when I accepted the Lord, and he's been a major part of my life ever since. By the time I was fifteen, I was very depressed and unhappy, but I kept on behaving the way I had been taught.

At sixteen I left the town and went to a Christian boarding school. I looked at it as a chance to get away from the community and start over. There I gained back some confidence, but I had a bad feeling inside, as if there was something wrong with me. I never finished high school; in fact, I felt as if I couldn't finish anything. Then I left and went to live with a relative in another province. There I got involved with a church group where I met lots of new friends and started to feel better about myself, but it was as if something was buried deep inside. Being away helped me discover activities that I enjoyed and talents that I never knew I had. I sang a lot. I just loved to sing.

I met the man who would be my husband when I was eighteen, and before long I was pregnant. We decided to get married quickly. Four months after we were married, Stan became angry at something. He raised his fist at me and said, "I could put your head right through that wall." I had never before seen that kind of violence and anger in a person's eyes. There was no anger in our home when I grew up, and I didn't know how to handle it. After that, I was always afraid of Stan. He would shout, criticize, ridicule, and call me names.

After the baby, Caroline, was born I had to go back to work because we were in financial trouble. Stan used to go out and spend our money on stuff for himself, even when there was no food for me and the baby. We moved so that he could find work. Then I got pregnant again. When I was nine months pregnant, he wanted me to help him move a fifteen-foot wooden boat. I said to him, "I can't lift it. I'm going to drop it." He said, "You drop it and you'll be sorry." He would threaten me with violence and threaten to destroy my possessions.

There were many "honeymoon" times when things calmed down and we had fun with the kids. At these times I'd start to feel optimistic that things would get better between us, and I'd try harder to please him. Then we moved back to the city. Caroline was six by then, and Derek was four. Stan hated Caroline and he always made her feel bad. She was quiet and gentle, and Stan had wanted sons that he could roughhouse with. He took to Derek and never even said "boo" to Caroline. I had another two children in less than three years: Martin and Sarah.

All this time I was involved in the life of the church while raising the children. I went to Bible studies and ladies' groups. Sometimes I'd sing at church, but Stan hated that. In fact, he was so much against it that I had to quit the singing. I just sang at home after that, but he'd get mad at me and tell me I had a terrible voice. I stopped singing.

Stan's spending habits were bad for our finances. He would treat himself to meals out when the kids and I had no money for food. Even when he wasn't working, he'd take all the money I earned and spend it on himself. I had trouble working and looking after everything. Whenever he came through the door, we'd all do his bidding. I didn't realize how much of a slave I had become, emotionally and physically. I did what he wanted because, if I didn't, he'd get mad and slap me across the small of the back. I'd work long into the night doing the household stuff. Then I'd be exhausted the next day, but I still had to go to work and take care of the kids. This went on for years, and as I got more and more exhausted, I was able to do less for Stan. This made him more angry and violent.

My participation in the church grew less because I had no energy. I pulled away from many things because, all of a sudden, I saw that we weren't a typical Christian family anymore, even though Stan was an elder in the church. He'd put a front on and then come home and treat me horribly.

To find comfort I turned to my relationship with God. At times this fuelled my hope that the "God of miracles" would change Stan into the father my children needed and the husband I longed for. I begged God to soften Stan's heart, help him to love me, and give him a sense of love and care for the children, particularly Caroline, whom he mocked and criticized relentlessly. Sometimes I experienced tremendous comfort when I sensed God close to me.

I used to think that if I could die, I'd go to be with Jesus. I thought about suicide many times. I guess my relationship with God prevented me from following through, because I always thought I might go to hell if I took my own life. I also knew that, if I did it, I'd have to take the children with me, because I could never think of dying and leaving them with Stan. The only one he was good to was Derek, probably because Derek was rough like himself. I could not think about divorce because I believed that marriage was "till death do us part." There were still some good times when Stan would be loving and he'd apologize. That would get me hoping for a miracle, and I'd begin to trust him again.

When the kids were between eight and seventeen, Stan got a new job with a lot of stress and he often failed to come home. Now I know that he'd found someone else, but at the time I just thought he was stressed. That's when the abuse got worse. He slapped me until I was black and blue. He'd pinch my breasts until they were covered with bruises. He'd slap me in front of the children and their friends, even in front of strangers. He didn't care who was nearby. For a long time there had been no laughter in the home. The children would cringe when Stan was around; and when he was absent, they would be troubled and angry. I had saved some money for Caroline to go to college. One day I came home and he said, "I spent the money on other stuff that we need more." I didn't know how I could replace the money. Caroline had to get another job to pay for college.

Finally, I talked to some women at church. They suggested that I should love him more so that God would change him; so I prayed more and tried harder. I prayed, read scriptures, and listened to Christian music. I loved the songs that spoke of God's love and care for his children, and I began to experience God's love in a new way. By this time I was putting up with severe beatings on a regular basis, but I'd keep hearing God's voice in my mind, telling me that I was cherished and special. I could never figure out, though, why I had to endure such brutal beatings if God loved me. Although I had been taught that marriage is for life, I kept thinking, "I can't keep loving him when I'm getting beat all the time." There was no one whom I could trust and speak to except God; so I drew closer to him in prayer.

I started to question Stan's fidelity. He would spend long periods of time away from home, and on returning he would become more violent than before. He raped me many times and kept telling me and Caroline that we were useless and worthless. He kept beating me too, leaving hand marks on my legs. Mostly he left Sarah alone, but he was so rude to Caroline that her friends stopped coming over. They said, "We can't stand the way your father treats you and your mother." He didn't take to Martin much. Martin would never talk about it, though, and he kept out of Stan's way, spending most of his time at the homes of friends.

I was a basket case. For a while I attended a twelve-step group, and that gave me the chance to listen to other women talk, and I started to believe that perhaps I did have other options. I also made friends with people who had experienced what I was going through. They let me talk and cry, and they helped me to see how bad my marriage was and that I did not have to let it continue.

Finally, I discovered that my suspicions were correct. Stan

had a lover. I asked him to stop seeing his lady friend, but he refused. He told me he would have both of us and I'd have to put up with it. He continued to rape me, and it got worse and worse as he became more angry toward me. I was so scared that I went to the pastor, who said he'd talk to Stan. Stan then apologized. He said he wanted the marriage to continue, and he promised to dump his lady friend. But that night he was the worst he'd ever been. I was afraid he was going to take his fists to me and not stop. Then he raped me. After that horrific nightmare, I knew I could not go on. I prayed and begged God for permission to end the marriage. I know I heard his voice saying that I should tell Stan to leave.

I felt as if I had to get the approval of a pastor, even though I had heard God myself. The pastor said I was right and that I should no longer stay because it was not safe; he said I should separate and get a restraining order. That night I said to Stan, "Don't ever come near me again. I want you to leave." Stan didn't even argue. The next day he sat around all day and said nothing. Then, before the kids came home from school, he loaded up all his things and left. It seemed easy. But the worst part was to come. It was the mental games that he played and still continues to play. He'd say that he'd pay me support for the kids and he never did. Or he'd say he'd help with things, but he never did. He'd say he cared about the kids, but he wouldn't ever contact them, and he didn't even want to talk to Derek.

After we had separated, I reluctantly turned to my family for help because I had no other resources left and was desperate. I expected to receive judgement and condemnation, but they rallied round, offering help with many things from work around the house to financial aid. At church, though, people were not supportive of the separation. Even friends stopped talking to me. It was as if I had committed a crime. I received tremendous help and support from people outside the church, such as neighbours and the twelve-step group. I grew close to two friends who offered help with daily tasks and were always there to listen. They continued to support me during the divorce process. I learned about ways to nurture myself, something I had never done before. I allowed myself to sing. I visited with friends, and I even went for a massage.

When Stan first left, I felt strong, but I had to keep busy so that I didn't think too much. People would say, "It's amazing how you're handling this." Then I started to fall apart, and memories of the rapes kept coming to mind. A counsellor insisted that I had to go back and deal with the original rape before I could deal with the stuff that happened in the marriage. The counsellor helped me see that I had to take care of myself and grieve for all the years that I had lost, all the family times that could have been, all the damage to my children. She helped me understand the dynamics of what had happened and recognize that it was not my fault. I leaned a lot on God, and he gave me peace of mind.

It seemed so unfair and unjust, though. Stan had a lot of stuff and plenty of money, but the kids and I had next to nothing. I would lie awake at night and wonder, "How am I going to put food on the table?" Fortunately my neighbours and friends were very helpful and helped me out when finances got low. People rallied round the kids and took them out with their own families. The counsellor helped me see that my needs are important and must be met in order for me to be a healthy mother for my kids. I discovered ways to meet my needs without leaning on anyone else. I also reached a point of forgiveness toward Stan. This did not come easily, but after the grieving I knew it was best for all of us to forgive.

Just recently, I sold off my house to pay the debts that Stan left me with. That's after five years in which he has never paid child support. I have not stopped leaning on God for comfort and provision. God has been a husband to me and a father to my children. I talk to the Lord just as if to another person. In the early years of the marriage God was just a spirit, but now he's real, and I sense his presence very powerfully. I still experience a lot of grief about the impact of the abuse on the children. They have little contact with Stan and feel deeply hurt by his rejection of them. It seemed as if Caroline was harmed more than the others, but it's Martin who has the most trouble now. He's into drinking. But I know they are healing. It's remarkable that Caroline is doing as well as she is, but she knows the Lord, and I think he has protected her from a lot.

For many years there was no laughter in our home, but the kids are all laughing again now, and it feels like I am coming alive again. Through all of this God has never left me. I visualize myself as a little child standing at the end of a tunnel. The Lord is holding my hand, and there's light at the other end. He says, "We've got to go through this tunnel, but you are not alone, I'm here with you." My relationship with God gave me a new appreciation of myself and showed me that I am valuable. It was the only thing that kept me going. He helped me see that I have a lot of talents. I have started to sing again, but my voice is different — deeper, fuller. I think it has a passion that comes from the Holy Spirit.

Chapter Eight

The Five L's of Leaving

After enduring many years in marriages where physical and emotional abuse left them with little self-esteem and confidence, the women eventually gained the strength needed to make new choices, and to leave their marriages.

Many patterns emerged in the final decisions of the women to divorce their mates, but these decisions all involved a lengthy, ever evolving, process of change and transformation. The journey to freedom was not easy for any of these courageous women, and for each one the journey continues.

1. Loosening denial

The women were more able to see their situations realistically after experiencing a loosening of denial. This occurred as they developed some self-awareness and acquired deeper insight into the nature of the abuse. The process usually involved reaching bottom, gaining insight, and finally reacting to isolation.

Reaching bottom

Each woman experienced a sense of hopelessness accompanied by the recognition that "I cannot do this anymore." Lily relates, "It's almost like I tried to compensate for collapsing on the inside with more of this external effort, until I reached the point of burnout and had nothing left; so I had to start addressing what needed to be changed." Several women considered ending their lives. Thoughts of suicide seemed to facilitate the acquisition of a new perspective. Barbara contemplated suicide many times, while others actually tried to take their lives. Lily states, "It had been six months that I had not seen my friends, and I was just deteriorating. Then the suicide attempt happened."

Each woman reached a point where she looked inside and discovered great debilitation. At this point, denial could no longer keep reality at bay. The husbands' alcohol abuse, love affairs, and emotional distancing served to escalate the violence and verbal abuse until the wives could no longer ignore the devastation. Reaching bottom resulted in the women ending their denial.

Most husbands withdrew emotionally, refusing to communicate their feelings, and some remained silent and aloof for days or weeks at a time. But distancing did not always mean silence. Some made jokes and lewd comments regardless of the seriousness of the discussion. All husbands exhibited tremendous anger. These behaviours too drove the wives to finally realize the extent of the family discord.

Children suffered greatly. Some were rejected by their fathers, while others experienced verbal and/or physical abuse, as did their mothers. Others became confused and depressed.

Seeing their children suffer caused the women to face their denial of the abuse. In some cases, sexual abuse prompted mothers to recognize the need to confront their husbands.

Gaining insight

Insight about the marriage occurred slowly and was often accompanied by a "spiritual awakening." The women "turned a corner" and came face to face with the ugliness of the situation, and suddenly a light went on. Marie was "shocked" by what she suddenly saw. Lily experienced an "internal shift," while Barbara "just stood there and said, 'I can no longer take this.'" They began to observe other families and discover that their own marriages were very different. This recognition brought a clearer understanding of the trauma in their lives. The extent of the difficulties could no longer be ignored.

Reaction to isolation

Severe isolation, although it eventually became unbearable, afforded the women time for prayer and reflection. In some cases husbands had forced isolation on their wives, and in all cases the women had relinquished activities and given up friendships to improve their marriages and keep their husbands happy.

2. Leaning on God

The women all at some time experienced a deepening awareness of spiritual matters and of being cared for by a greater power. They turned to God, whom they all conceived in masculine terms. With the realization that the husband could not meet his wife's needs, came the discovery that a husband can never fill the void created by childhood abandonment. God then replaced husbands as the subject of devotion.

Lessening dependency on the husband

Hurting and desperate, the women sought affirmation, approval, and support from their husbands. When, over a long period of time, this was not forthcoming, the women began to depend more on God and stopped looking to their husbands for emotional fulfillment. This enabled them to open themselves to the experience of healing as a gift from God.

Turning to God during isolation

During periods of extreme isolation, the women turned to God. Prayer and meditation met their need for communication in which they could be honest and real. As such communication deepened, tolerance for the abuse grew weaker.

Developing a relationship with God

The process of developing a relationship with God had started before the marriage. However, all the woman experienced distancing from God as they increased their efforts to gain the love of their husbands. They hoped that God's love for them would involve a miracle to change their husbands. During the period of reawakening, they discarded this "magical thinking," realizing that they could make their own choices under the guidance of God. Some heard an audible voice telling them they were "worthy," "important," or "God's precious child." Some sensed God saying that he loved them and did not want them to be mistreated.

The rediscovery of self-worth enabled each woman to become more honest with God about the abuse. Some were angry and blamed God for allowing it. Some were confused about why God allowed them to suffer. Others feared that they might have displeased God. Expressing deep concerns to God provided a new freedom and allowed them to experience acceptance by him. For some, this was the first time in their lives that they had felt accepted.

Through this process each woman was able to appreciate herself and to comprehend the severity of the abuse. As dependency was transferred from husband to God, the women grew stronger in the resolve to break the control of the relationship.

Seeing God in different ways

Equipped with new knowledge and insight, the women could distinguish between their spiritual experiences and the legalism of the church's teachings. God could now be viewed as loving and healing instead of punitive and legalistic. For some, God ceased to be a distant God — "out there somewhere" — and felt close as healer. Viewing God as healer instead of judge allowed for a re-evaluation of certain biblical interpretations that had served to keep the women in bondage, and provided a new perspective on the marriage. The women could see that God was not a stern judge who hated divorce and demanded that the marriage continue at any cost to the women, but was a healer who desired their health and wholeness. They derived strength from trusting God to lead them out of the abuse, despite being fearful and uncertain as to what that would involve.

A relationship in which one individual is dependent on another to meet all their needs, including those that derive from childhood, is not healthy. In such cases, an imbalance of power exists. When the women were able to transfer this dependency from their husbands to God, their eyes were opened and they were able to be realistic about the deficits in the relationship. Thus, the women experienced a new sense of freedom from the confines of the abuse, and each one could then be open to the idea that God would want to lead her away from the abuse.

3. Learning about self

Learning about self brings an increased awareness of one's own capabilities and potential, through grieving losses and identifying problems experienced in the original family.

Identifying and grieving losses

In most cases the grieving process was initiated by awareness of the damage done to the children. The women experienced extraordinary guilt around the failure to provide a comfortable safe home for the children. Other wounds were acknowledged, such as those that occurred in the women's own childhoods. Disappointed dreams of what a family is supposed to be spawned anger, sorrow, and discouragement. Most became aware that they had never experienced a nurturing environment in either marriage or childhood.

Grieving enabled the women to become open to embracing the pain of multiple losses. They could then move toward accepting their wounds and take steps toward making new choices.

Gaining insight into problems in the original family

Experiences in the women's original families had contributed to their tolerance of abuse. Through grieving, they could see how the early family experiences had impacted on adult decisions. Lack of nurturing in childhood resulted in their becoming adults with childhood needs that had never been met. Some felt they were set up for disastrous marriages because of the emotional abandonment they experienced in childhood when their needs for affirmation, comfort, understanding, and unconditional positive regard were not met. Often such relationship patterns can be seen in several generations, as individuals repeat the dynamics experienced in the home. Once the women recognized unhealthy patterns in their families, they were better able to gain a sense of themselves as individuals apart from those families and to begin to nurture themselves.

Appreciating oneself

An inward journey of self-discovery helped the women acknowledge their needs and examine their attitudes, private myths, and marriage vows. They began to value themselves and to identify and define the abuse, realizing that it was wrong and undeserved. Thus, they could relinquish what they had imagined was their own responsibility for the abuse, develop respect for their own positive qualities, and resolve to stop the abusive cycle.

Developing a sense of self apart from, and in relation to, God

The women began to integrate their spiritual experiences with their perceptions of themselves. The view of God as loving healer became integrated with the view of themselves as having gifts and abilities that could be used to generate an income. This permitted them to make the final move toward leaving the marriage. Inner strength came from spiritual experiences and self-discovery, and provided a sense of empowerment that resulted in a new vision of self and the awareness that it was time to leave.

4. Listening to others

As the women opened up to others they all received wise counsel. Sometimes help came from friends, other times from pastors or counsellors. These encounters provided bridging relationships and elicited new input.

Opening up to others

After many years of isolation and abuse, all the women began to trust others and make friends. Usually this was a slow process that occurred over several years. Support groups and networks afforded the opportunity to form new friendships and establish relationships with others who were also struggling with difficult situations. In some cases, women from within the church were available to listen and not judge. All the women were eventually able to confide in someone and to talk about the abuse. Thus, they experienced validation and support.

Encouraging family responses

Despite the fear of being judged, the women found someone in the family in whom to confide. Relatives offered emotional and also concrete support. In many cases, families had suspected severe problems but had felt helpless and confused about what action to take. They expressed relief at finally gaining some answers and explanations.

Supportive and mutual friendships

Friendships offered needed support for the women to take a realistic look at the marriage. They were able to gain new perspectives and to see that the lives of others were different from their own. Friendships enabled the women to receive new information that helped them become aware of the extent of the abuse. They could talk about their experiences, gain strength and encouragement from others, and then consider alternative solutions to the problems within their marriages. Ultimately they could withdraw from the tumultuous relationship with the husband. Helpful networks included support groups, friends, neighbours, community groups, Bible study groups, and church activity groups.

Counselling

Validating and supportive counselling provided safety and an opportunity to gain a new perspective. In some cases counselling provided an antidote to the exhortations of pastors to save the marriage at any cost. Counselling also gave the women the opportunity to heal and grieve, and to work through the pain suffered in childhood and marriage. Some women who had experienced suicidal thoughts found that talking to a counsellor helped to put these thoughts into perspective. Some of the women signed a contract with the counsellor stating that, instead of harming themselves, they would first call the counsellor to talk. Where depression was evident, some women needed medical intervention in the form of anti-depressants in order to gain the emotional strength to deal with their pain.

Counsel from pastors

Three women reported seeking guidance from pastors who offered validation and support. One pastor, who possessed knowledge of family violence, proved very helpful, while another reinforced a victim's perceptions of the marriage and helped her to see that it had ended, emotionally, years before. In some cases, pastors who were consulted after the decision to end the relationship provided the final validation needed to pursue the separation process.

5. Letting go and making changes

While still in the marriages the women started to take risks and make changes. They let go of their dreams about having the ideal family with their husband and replaced these with new dreams and goals. Some changes involved developing self-nurturing behaviours. Some of the women discovered or rediscovered the things that brought them joy, such as dancing, singing, or being with children. Some finally felt free to take time for themselves, such as going for a massage, reading the Bible, spending time with friends, joining a choir, or taking a class.

Responding differently to situations

The women learned to be open with others and to trust. Some were able to break old patterns of reaction to their families. All broke the old patterns of reacting to their husbands by detaching themselves, refusing to get drawn into conflict or needless debates, and ceasing to apologize for their actions. This resulted in a greater sense of independence and strength.

Trying new tasks and developing new interests

As the women felt better about themselves they took on new challenges that provided greater feelings of well-being and precipitated more changes that, in turn, led to the development of new interests and increased self-esteem. The resulting confidence in their abilities made it possible for the women to effect important life changes. One woman took up dancing, another joined a choir, while yet another made a significant career change. The women all experienced the benefits of nurturing themselves. Through counselling and support groups they developed strategies to nurture and care for themselves by identifying their needs and taking steps to meet those needs.

Joining a new church

Soon after separating from their husbands, many of the women began attending different churches where they felt validated and accepted. These new contacts enabled them to make new friends and develop other interests. They selected church bodies where there was an emphasis on welcoming single parents, or where attention was paid to the needs of those who were suffering.

Chapter Nine

Opal

*"I knew when I left
that I was stopping
three or four generations
of dysfunction."*

I was the result of an unwanted pregnancy. My parents did not want me, and they told me so. Living with this abandonment has left a wound inside me, an empty heart that only God can heal. I always felt estranged from my mother; her rejection of me has been constant and still continues today.

We had a very strict family life without much feeling of being close. My father was authoritarian. He controlled and tyrannized the family. He set lots of rules such as what time to come in and who I could spend time with. I was the over-responsible child who tried to please and to earn the love I desperately needed. I did well in school, and therefore I was constantly reminded that I was to be an example, since I would be the only one in the family who made anything of herself. My father looked to me to carry the expectations of the family. I was very unhappy. In spite of the many rules, my family did not seem to care about each other. My parents used to fight a lot, and they'd try to make the children side with one or the other. We attended church regularly, but I wasn't a Christian or anything, although I had a very strong belief in God, and I knew I wanted to go to heaven.

When I was about fifteen, I got involved with the young people's organization at a local church, and I started to see myself as more than just an unhappy person in an unhappy family. I started to see my life differently, and I felt happier. My father even allowed me to get rides to the church group because he thought it was a good thing for me to get so involved in church. Through this group I met Jerry, and we began dating when I was fifteen. He was my first date, and we continued to date while I took career training. I had a need to be needed: that's why I wanted to be in a helping profession. I had learned that I could get approval by being helpful and taking care of others. When I met Jerry, he was very much a wounded duck. He was very introverted and quiet, and came from a very strict evangelical family that didn't give him much approval; so I felt drawn to reach out to help him.

When I got pregnant, Jerry and I decided to marry. As I look back, I see there was some love between us, but it was the wrong kind of love. I probably got married so that I could resist my father and his control. While we were dating, I did not see the other side of Jerry. I had been studying much of the time, and we had not spent a great deal of time together; and when we were together, there was always a lot to do. In the first two weeks of marriage, Jerry changed completely. He would have nothing more to do with church. He had started to drink before we married, but I did not realize how heavily. He had also taken to going out with the guys a lot of the time, but I had not been aware of how much.

I became busy with the new baby, and after I stopped nursing, I became pregnant again right away, and I went on to have three more children in the following four years. Jerry did not help at all with any of the parenting. I had to do it all on my own, and the only model I had was my own family. So I did what I was used to. I became very strict. I hated the way my dad brought me up, and I did not want to be like him, but that was the only way I knew. Jerry was very demanding. He seemed jealous of the time I gave the children and tried to monopolize my time. It was as if I had a fifth child, my husband, who needed me, but I was too busy with the other children to have time for him.

Those first ten years of the marriage were about mere survival. Jerry drank very heavily and didn't come home until very late when the children were in bed. He would have outbursts of anger, call me names, criticize me, ridicule me, and put me down. Whenever he was home, he wanted me to give to him. I felt angry and resentful. I was often angry at the kids. There were many times when I resented them for tying me down because I believed that, if I were more available to Jerry, the marriage would be better.

In order to block out the abuse, I put my energy into raising the children and attending church activities. I walked with the Lord but in a superficial way. I was involved always in Bible studies and "Ladies' Time Out," and I even led Bible studies. I constantly wore a mask to show people that things were okay.

Things were not okay, however. I'd go home to Jerry's criticisms and angry tirades. His emotional outbursts alternated with extreme dependency. He was unable to be a father to the children and needed more mothering than they did. He needed me to be available constantly, and when I was busy with the children, he would be angry and moody. Then he would go and drink. He was needy and distant at the same time. I used to have the same dream again and again: he was in the area, and everybody could see him except me. I never had a dream in which I found him. In real life I felt very alone.

I started to draw away from my friends more and more. Although I felt depressed, I could not tell them. Nobody knew what went on in our home. Nobody knew Jerry was a drinker. I had always felt a sense of abandonment, and this was emphasized in the marriage. I did not believe I was worthwhile or that I deserved Jerry's love. I kept turning to God and praying for him to help me to keep going through the endless days of fatigue and depression. I leaned on the Lord for my strength, and he answered in a quiet way. I sensed his love and care. I begged him to heal the marriage and give me strength to keep loving Jerry in a way that would see him change.

The second ten years of the marriage were a time of denial. My friendships were characterized by distance and superficiality. I constantly had to wear a mask so that no one would find out that Jerry drank. He also played cards and gambled, and he hung around with others who did the same; so he hardly ever came home. He would not share my desire to be in the church, and even that became painful for me. When he was around, Jerry would criticize and berate me. He would often get violently mad, but he never actually hit me, although once he tore my clothes. He would put me down or use passive resistance, such as not doing anything or not communicating with me in any way, and often he just did not come home.

The church taught that the husband should be a spiritual leader, but Jerry was not there. I tried to escape into busy-ness, but it was terribly exhausting because I had to raise the children as well. I sang in the choir and continued my involvement in as many church activities as I could handle. I'd practise my singing at home, but Jerry would yell at me to stop the awful noise. Eventually I did confide in two friends, but I told them only a little bit about my situation, just so that they could pray. I did not level with them because I felt so ashamed of what was going on.

Exhausted and worn down, I kept turning to God for the strength to continue. For many years I communicated with God only about the abuse because I had no energy even to talk about other things or to pray for others. One day God answered by directing me to Al-Anon. I had a neighbour who had been beaten by her husband, and she was going to Al-Anon; so I went with her. It was very refreshing to meet others who related similar experiences and listened without judging. I mentioned to Jerry that I had been there and that perhaps we should get help for our marriage. He became very angry and said I should never bring up our dirty laundry in front of other people.

After that I didn't say I was going to Al-Anon, but I would sneak out because the support I received there became so important. I learned ways of detaching from the situation. But although I could accept that the drinking was a disease for other people, I could not accept that it was a disease for Jerry. I still believed that he liked what he was doing and could stop it if he wanted. I continued with Al-Anon because there was greater safety there than in the church. I could risk trusting these people, whereas the church did not seem safe. I had observed people who attempted to trust at church, and I had seen how they were condemned.

I gradually developed a relationship with a woman from Al-Anon. She was going through the same things as I was with a husband who drank much of the time and treated her badly. We bonded. I could call her any time and talk to her, and she would reinforce that it was all right for me to feel bad or angry. We became real supports for each other and have continued our friendship over the years. We're closer than sisters now. I found that talking to her helped me gain strength. Through our conversations I realized that other people's lives were not like mine. I did a lot of grieving for the family that had never been, and I experienced much pain over the losses of my children.

In the last five years of the marriage, Jerry's drinking consumed him. We had no set supper hours. Friday night he would be gone all night, and often he did not come home all day Saturday. I was not allowed to ask where he was because it would make him really angry. He'd say he was glad I was a Christian because it meant that I could not leave him. In the last three years, I began to suspect that he was involved with someone else, but when I'd question him, he would not answer. Then one night when he came home from drinking, he woke me up and confessed that he'd been with someone else, but he went on to say that he still wanted the marriage to work.

After that, I talked with the Lord, and I went to a retreat centre to think and pray. There I spoke with a pastor who was very helpful. I listened to the Lord, and the Lord told me how much he loved me. The Lord also told me that he loved Jerry too and wanted Jerry to change. I returned home feeling that I should be not angry but gentle and forgiving toward Jerry. When I tried to talk to him about love and God's love, he actually started to share his feelings and to tell me about the pain he was in, but suddenly he just closed off and said no more. I think it was just too frightening for him to share his pain. That was the closest I would ever get to him.

Jerry continued to drink and gamble so heavily that he was gone most of the time except maybe a day and a half each week. Finally, I figured it all out. It was as if the Lord spoke very clearly and told me what was happening. I realized he had been having an affair for several years and that, when he failed to come home, he was staying with another woman. Through this time I had been talking to my friend and doing more things for myself. I was living a life without Jerry, and recognizing this helped me to gain strength and confidence in myself. Eventually, I was strong enough to do what I had to do — end the marriage — and the Lord gave me the courage to do it. Although it was not easy, it seemed a routine thing when it actually happened. I simply said, "I want you out. I want a divorce. I want to get on with my life because we are no good for each other and that's the way it is." Then I packed his stuff, and he left without arguing or anything.

When I informed the pastor of what had happened, he apologized for not giving me the support that I needed. At that time the church that I attended condemned divorce. The stigma of divorce was very strong, and there were many people in the church who shunned me. The shame was heavy, and I worried about what people were saying and thinking. After a short while I changed churches and started on a very intense healing journey during which I received extensive counselling and attended many recovery groups.

These activities helped me to work through my own family issues and to see how I had become involved with a person like Jerry in the beginning. The difficult relationship with my father had left me needing the approval of men. I got self-esteem through rescuing people, and when I met Jerry, he desperately needed to be rescued. It took me until the end of the marriage to realize that I could not rescue him from himself, and I could not even penetrate the wall that he had erected. I learned ways to heal from my original family problems by grieving for what

I never had as a child. I learned to heal from the marriage through grieving, nurturing myself, and developing new ways to relate to people, rather than always needing to rescue someone.

Some of the ways I nurtured myself were through listening to music, taking time to pray, and spending quality time with friends, where we no longer wore masks and made small talk but actually shared our joys and sorrows together. The support groups were very important. There I could share my pain with others who knew the same kind of pain. This was a great source of strength and healing. I developed new friendships and strengthened ties with friends who had not rejected me.

Although it was a lot of work, I knew God was with me at every turn. I spent hours in prayer and worship, drawing strength from the Lord. Through the process of prayer and working through the terrible pain of the marriage, I was able to forgive Jerry, and I now have no resentment or anger toward him. I give God the whole glory for what I came through and for giving me a second chance at life. God has been there all along, giving me love and showing me care.

God also gave me a chance to rebuild relationships with my children. I still grieve for my children because of how they were brought up. They were hurt so badly because of the absence of their father, because of the way I tried to parent them alone, and because of the times that I was unable to listen because I was pouring so much energy into worrying about Jerry and our marriage. They are now getting help for their pain but it will be a lengthy journey for each of them. I knew when I left my husband that I was changing the pattern of a very dysfunctional family. My grandparents had a terrible relationship and my great-grandparents had an even worse one. I realize now that my relationship with Jerry was not successful because I had not had a successful relationship with my father. I see how much I have needed to trust in my heavenly father because I had not been able to trust in men.

Jerry and I are divorced, and our children have grown up. I am now married to a wonderful man whom I met at church. We are working together, my husband and I, in missions. I realize that the healing work I did after the divorce, and the healing that I have received through my relationship with the Lord, is what prepared me for this marriage.

The Lord has made us all very intricate and very interesting, and his unconditional love is something I grasp more and more. I am now very involved in the life of a new church. I helped to establish groups for divorced Christians, and I am running groups for the children of divorce. The Lord has used me to develop a ministry to those wounded by abuse and divorce.

Chapter Ten

Hope for Healing

The home is a place where one expects to find safety, and Christian homes, where family members espouse the teachings of Christ, are especially likely to be considered places of refuge. Unfortunately for numerous Christian women, the home is a dangerous place — a place of lost dreams, broken health, and shattered hopes for a refuge in which to raise children who love God. The women presented here endured terrible experiences and multiple losses and yet they retained their religious values and their belief in God. Despite the fact that each woman's journey was highly individual, many common themes and patterns emerged out of their stories.

Family dynamics may lead to abusive relationships

Before discussing the ingredients of healing, it is helpful to look at the way in which the family dynamics identified by the women concur with literature dealing with abusive marital relationships.

The following is a summary of the general family structure and emotional cycle, as identified by Barbara Pressman (1989), that characterizes an abusive family. Pressman does not explain the abuse, but describes the structure that exists, outlining situational factors as follows:

1. The husband is controlling in order to get his needs met.
2. The wife is demoted in the executive adult hierarchy and, because of the abuse, emotionally withdraws. She may do her husband's bidding and try to please him; however, because of the abuse and fear, she cannot feel close to him.
3. The husband isolates his wife from friends, relatives, and contacts outside the family.
4. The children are "parentified," as parents seek nurturing from children who need to be taken care of themselves. While providing protection and comfort, these children often become equal, in status, to mothers.
5. The family is isolated from community involvement and outside resources. Children are reluctant to bring friends home.
6. Families maintain secrecy about the abuse.
7. The husband believes he cannot live without his wife and often threatens suicide if she talks of leaving. The spouse believes she must stay to prevent him from harming himself. She loses her strength and confidence in her ability to care for herself and believes she cannot survive without her husband.

Pressman posits that these dynamics occur in all families, Christian and otherwise.

Formula for freedom

Just as the family lives of the women in this study conform to the pattern that Pressman identifies, so, she notes (pp. 25–27), do their journeys toward healing.

1. The women began attending to their own safety, acknowledging that they have a right to care about themselves.
2. They realized that they are not to blame for the violence of others.
3. Denial and minimization were abandoned as coping strategies. The women ceased telling themselves, "He means well," "At least he didn't hit me," or "It's not as bad as it could be."
4. They developed coping strategies that were not self-destructive or harmful to children, but that afforded support, safety, and enhanced self-esteem.
5. They challenged the societal and religious myths and expectations that insist on women remaining in abusive relationships and blame them for doing so.
6. They developed an awareness of their strengths, skills, and competence and used this awareness to take risks and explore new behaviours.
7. They were able to reestablish a sense of power over their own lives, overcoming the belief that they are helpless and powerless. This helped them to lessen their dependency on husbands as providers.
8. A sense of self-worth developed as they recognized that they have the right to express their own needs and to satisfy them. This led to an appreciation of themselves and to recognition of their importance to God.

9. They were able to recognize feelings of helplessness and connect those feelings with the experience of being abused, with the socialization of women, and with the religious context that discriminates against women.
10. They established a social network whereby isolation and family secrecy are overcome.
11. They learned to express feelings of victimization, especially rage and anger, without feeling inhuman, unfeminine, or disloyal.
12. They recognized and articulated the ambivalence they felt toward their abusers, who were not monsters, were not always abusive, and in some cases possessed many endearing qualities.
13. They were able to deal with grief and loss around the separation.
14. They recognized that they were capable of making good decisions and choices.
15. They reconciled their religious beliefs with a new view of God and his ability to love them.

Religion is not the determining issue in abusive relationships

The findings of the study agree with much of the literature that discusses abuse among non-Christian couples. Many people think that religious teaching is the cement that keeps a Christian woman bound to her husband. However, the literature indicates that, in addition to religious teachings, Christian women experience the impact of the same multiplicity of variables that work together to keep non-Christian women bound.

It is further evident that the healing process results from much more than simply reframing biblical teachings about marriage and divorce. For these women, healing occurred over a lengthy period and was characterized by many elements all working in combination to assist them in their efforts to extricate themselves from fear.

A common assumption of many Christians is that God can free them from their pain and trials with some miraculous wave of his hand. But the truth is less simple. God is a loving God, devoted to the well-being of each person. God knows the path that each must take to experience freedom and wholeness, and that time is needed for a person to confidently tread a new path and develop new ways of being in the world. God knows that each woman's journey is unique.

Every person who has experienced abuse will walk a different journey to healing. For some, the path may be long and winding with many detours. For others, the path may be straight and direct. Although previous chapters have identified many common themes in the individual journeys, each individual walks her own path to freedom. This chapter provides an outline of what is required for deep healing and change to take place. Although transformation may take years of struggle, any who desire to grow will eventually experience freedom. In order to heal from an abusive marriage, the abused woman needs to take responsibility for the process of change and transformation, and to embrace this process.

Exodus from denial

Jesus says, "You will know the truth, and the truth will set you free" (John 8:32). Dan Allender (1990) in *The Wounded Heart* describes how denial keeps an abused individual from experiencing reality and discusses the way that abuse victims must break through denial in order to be set free (199ff). God knows that to live in lies and secrecy is to be bound by deception. Women who live in abusive marriages deny the truth in order to tolerate the abuse. They are then forced to construct a world of lies that requires a tremendous output of energy to keep it in place.

In contrast, honesty is the commitment to see reality as it is and to live in the here and now. When a woman lives in honesty, she allows the truth to free her from the burden of living in a false world. Honesty lifts the huge load from her shoulders, and enables her to experience the relief of finally coming face to face with her situation, including the abuse from which she has been running. As she moves away from denial and into reality, she often experiences the following process, similar to that described by Allender with regard to victims of sexual abuse. She cycles through these stages, sometimes repeatedly, although not necessarily in this order:

1. She acknowledges that she has been abused.
2. She recognizes that the abuse has damaged her.
3. She sees that the abuse has damaged her children.
4. She realizes that it will take time to deal with the process of healing.
5. She acknowledges the destructive impact of keeping the secret of the abuse hidden behind a veil of shame and sees the need to share her experience with others with whom she can feel safe.
6. She recognizes that she has developed self-protective behaviours to insulate her from the pain of abuse, and becomes

aware of the way in which these have impacted on her relationships with herself and others.

Entering a relationship with God that results in repentance and forgiveness

In order to become free from her captivity, the abused woman lets go of her idealized husband and turns to God, replacing her husband as the centre of her world with a God who loves her and wants to provide for her in a way she deserves. Her dependency on an unpredictable man is lessened. She will cease to wonder constantly what he is doing, where he is, or what mood he will be in when he comes home. Her thoughts are directed away from her husband and toward God, and also toward her own needs. The process of learning to depend on God begins with getting to know God. Prayer draws us into God's presence and invites God into our life. Reading the Bible allows us to become aware of God's concerns and intentions. As this occurs, the abused woman is able to talk to God and listen, responding deep within her spirit. When she connects with God in such a deep way, she embarks on the road to repentance and forgiveness.

Repentance occurs when we identify aspects of our behaviour that have impacted adversely on our lives. For many who have suffered abuse, these behaviours take the form of self-protective measures that keep a person distant from others. According to Allender, repentance occurs when we recognize that "… our self-protective means to avoid hurt have not ushered us into real living (the reckless abandon to God that ultimately leads to a deep sense of wholeness and joy) or to purposeful, powerful relating" (217, 218). Repentance requires acknowledging that these defences keep us isolated and distant from others, thus denying us the opportunity to engage in the intimacy of healing relationships.

Forgiveness occurs when we realize that we are ready to relinquish blaming the abuse on the other person. When we hold resentment against the abuser, we damage ourselves by pouring great energy into angry thoughts of getting even. Forgiveness frees us from that anger and allows us to rechannel our energy into loving ourselves and others. Then we can invest in relationships that heal. True forgiveness does not mean that we allow ourselves to continue being abused or that we re-enter an abusive relationship. It means that we give up the right to hold it against the person and we let go of our hatred and anger. This can occur as we develop a relationship with a loving, caring God.

Discovering oneself

The abused woman has lived in a world of denial, afraid to face life and to recognize the abuse. As she relinquishes denial, she is forced to embrace truth and to look at who she is. The journey to look realistically at oneself is accompanied by deep grief as she faces the many losses that have been incurred. The grief is exacerbated as she realizes that her current situation is often the result of childhood events that contributed to her propensity to enter such a relationship.

Once denial has been broken, the grieving person often experiences a combination of anger, bargaining, and depression. Anger is a healthy response to injustice and a valid response to the violations one has suffered. Bargaining is about the chance to make things the way we wish they could be. For the abused wife, it involves asking God for another chance, begging God to change her spouse, telling herself that if only she had prayed more, been a better wife, or tried harder, things would have worked out. Bargaining is a normal part of the process of coming to terms with losses. Depression involves the sadness and mourning that are experienced as the abused person recognizes that her many dreams have been shattered, damage has been done to her and her children, and many of these losses are permanent. The depression cannot be short circuited. It has to run its course.

After cycling and recycling through these stages, the woman eventually reaches a level of acceptance regarding the abuse and its consequences. In so doing, she achieves a level of freedom from the anger and sorrow about what has happened. She is ready to move on to pursue her own goals and dreams with a measure of joy. Acceptance does not, however, mean that the woman no longer has any sadness or other feelings around the abuse. She will continue to experience waves of grief for many years, but these grieving episodes are likely to be brief, sporadic, and of lessening intensity. They will be quite different from the energy-draining, all-consuming grief episodes that are experienced in the early stages.

In order to become free from the bondage of abuse and to develop a sense of self, the abused woman must reclaim her past by allowing memories of the abuse to surface and be validated. Often abused individuals try to forget their experiences and remove them from their consciousness. This only intensifies the harm such repressed memories can do because, when we remove experiences from memory, we cut off parts of our self. By recognizing the past, we free ourselves to be all that we are. Facing the past enables us to see the present more clearly and frees us from any hidden secrets that have the potential to spring out and expose us as flawed. As an individual remembers the nature of the abuse that occurred within the marriage, she begins to gain insight into her situation. With insight comes knowledge and understanding that, no matter how painful, eventually free the individual and promote healing. Expressing feelings about the abuse allows the individual to be honest about herself and her experiences.

As the woman identifies the abuse in her marriage, she gains insight into her original family and identifies issues that might have predisposed her to enter a marriage that was less than nurturing. Childhood experiences had considerable impact on the ways these women dealt with relationships. Murray Bowen (1978) observes that people are shaped by their family's emotional processes and ways of relating, and issues that have not been addressed in the original family affect future relationships. By examining relationship dynamics and the types of behaviours used for coping, the woman is able to get a sense of herself in relation to her original family. This helps as she grapples with the intensity of recognizing the flaws in her marriage.

An essential part of the process is to identify and recognize unmet childhood needs that may have driven her into such a relationship. Once these are identified, they must be healed so that she will no longer be propelled toward men like her former husband. To heal from childhood wounds, the woman will need to grieve her childhood losses, no matter how small or large. By grieving them she frees herself to move out of a state of powerlessness into a place where she can view herself as a worthwhile person. This involves renewing the mind and changing false assumptions that she may have had of herself as not worthy of respect and consideration.

Self-discovery leads the woman to face the ineffectiveness of previous survival behaviours that she used to defend herself against violations of self-esteem. These self-protective behaviours, such as remaining isolated from others, need to be replaced by new more trusting behaviours, and the woman will need to learn to recognize where it is safe to experiment. This will require her to trust her inner instincts. A woman's inner sense of good and bad, healthy and unhealthy, becomes distorted when she is in a close relationship where her decisions and choices are constantly challenged and ridiculed. She must now trust her instincts and develop confidence in her ability to make decisions.

As the abused person gains insight into her childhood wounds, into the abuse and the many losses that have resulted from the abuse, she will establish an emotional boundary around herself and will learn about who she is. She will begin to understand and cherish her relationship with God, becoming a whole person while still depending on God for strength.

Communicate with others

In order to heal from the trauma of abuse, a woman needs to have a support network around her. Although the path to freedom is an individual journey, trusted people can share the burden. When we have been constantly shamed and violated, we develop deep wounds that we want to protect. These places are raw and tender and we will not readily expose them to others who might harm us all over again. Therefore, the abused individual is reluctant to trust and let others into those tender places. However, although other people have caused such harm, other people also have the potential to effect healing by listening, validating, allowing for the expression of feelings without judging, and affirming the woman's attempts to heal.

For communication with others to be a healing experience, the abused person must communicate in an honest and authentic way. This means being honest about who she is. When communication is honest, we expose the past and reveal our shame. We allow another to fully experience with us. We are able to engage in reality testing when we honestly relate our experiences to another and experience his or her responses. Such communication is essential in the move toward freedom and trust.

Communication with a group of others who have experienced similar traumas is therapeutic in that it allows deep wounds to be dealt with among those who have been through similar experiences. Many forms of social support are helpful, ranging from friends and prayer partners to support groups and counsellors.

Open up to change

Change for the woman trying to heal from abuse will involve learning to take care of herself. Self-care has often been overlooked and assigned minimal importance during the marriage, and involves being open to new experiences, trying different behaviours, learning new things, and establishing clear boundaries.

Self-defeating attitudes also need to be identified and changed. One such attitude is that of too-easy forgiveness. Often people feel the pressure to forgive quickly. They may hurry to do this before they are ready, thus failing to forgive from the heart. Feelings of hurt, rage, and distrust must first be dealt with. The process of coming to forgiveness is a lengthy one that results from grieving, working through feelings, and processing the effects of the abuse with the help of a God who understands, loves, and accepts the individual.

Strategies that may have been used for self-protection may no longer be useful. Some individuals use dissociation to cut themselves off from the pain and the reality of the situation. While this strategy may have been useful during the marriage and while it may have been a contributor in moving the individual to seek help, it is not a behaviour that can help the woman obtain emotional health. Such strategies result in an individual remaining closed off emotionally from others and render her unable to experience real and deep emotion.

It is imperative to take time for the things that bring enjoyment and to do the things one never had time for in the past. Those who have to work and raise young children might find themselves exhausted and with little time even for sleep. Yet fun and joy are so necessary for healing that the exhausted woman needs to discover friends who can help with child care or find other single parents interested in establishing a support network where each helps the other. Support networks are crucial to the healing process. Women who have been isolated in difficult marriages need to develop relationships with others, where they can gain new information, witness healthy marital relationships, receive strength and encouragement, and experience a new reality.

Once out of the marriage the woman needs the help of others to maintain a healing perspective and to derive strength and encouragement to continue her focus on recovery from the trauma. Churches and communities offer women's groups, Bible studies, support groups, activity groups, and classes. All these can provide the opportunity for a woman to meet others with whom she can develop trust. Some churches offer twelve step groups for those who have difficult marital or family issues. Women's shelters provide information and support.

Taking care of oneself involves building and maintaining healthy boundaries. On the physical level, we need to have a physical boundary that determines who we will allow to come physically close to us and what kind of physical contact we will tolerate. On the emotional level, we need an emotional boundary that determines what type of behaviour we will tolerate from others and also how we will behave. Just as our physical space changes depending on who we are with, so does our emotional space. We will not stand as close to the salesperson in a store as we would to a very close friend. We allow some friends to hug us but not others. The same is true on an emotional level. We will not tell our deepest problems to the store clerk, but we may disclose very personal things to a close friend.

For the women in this study, there was little modelling in regard to the establishment of boundaries. They had either built walls or possessed very weak ineffective boundaries. As children, they had not been afforded the opportunity to experience healthy boundaries in their families. When children's boundaries and rights are invaded, they are forced into inappropriate roles with those around them. When they have been emotionally or physically neglected, abandoned, humiliated, or shamed, they may develop weak or non-existent boundaries and as adults are likely to be vulnerable to invasion.

In order to heal, it is necessary for a woman to take a look at how boundaries operated in the original family. Did parents invade her boundaries by constantly telling her what to do, how to be, or what to think? Did she constantly feel shamed and humiliated? Or did parents have rigid boundaries where each family member felt cut off from the others? As healing occurs from the wounds caused by unhealthy boundaries, it is important to begin establishing healthy boundaries that protect the person from unwanted behaviour. Healthy boundaries allow people to decide what behaviours they will or will not tolerate from others and to set limits on these.

How the church can help

Churches need to educate people about abuse. Church leaders themselves need to become educated about abuse issues. Until churches know and understand the nature of abuse, they will be of little assistance to abused people. Part of the education process involves recognizing the role that the church has played through interpretations of scripture and doctrine that cause women to stay in unhealthy situations and cause church leaders to counsel them to do so. Until very recently, men have been the ones to decide how the church views marriage, divorce, and abuse, and how a woman should respond to an abusive marriage.

Within the church, education about wife abuse must be preventative in nature, acknowledging that abuse does exist and helping Christians to recognize and identify its occurrence.

Youth in the church need to be educated about abuse and trained in communication skills. Girls must be helped to develop a sense of self that can stand alone. They must be taught that they do not need a man in order to be happy.

Men in church leadership positions are accustomed to viewing marriage and life from a position of control; therefore, they need to be educated regarding Christ's role as servant leader so that they can better comprehend the Ephesians chapter that exhorts husbands to love their wives as Christ loved the church.

Leaders in the church, and those who take a role in

caring for suffering members, need to recognize that abuse happens, even within the Christian marriage. They must then respond from a non-judgemental position where they are able to validate and affirm the abused spouse's responses and perceptions, instead of suggesting that she is imagining or exaggerating.

Although a primary role of the church is to facilitate reconciliation, it is important to recognize the danger of pushing for reconciliation when the circumstances indicate that the abuse is continuing. Education can help church leaders to know when reconciliation is appropriate and when it is not.

The church can and should accept an important role in directing both spouses toward counselling. The abuser needs help and the abused wife needs counselling. In many cases, temporary separation is advisable in order for each spouse to pursue individual healing free from the volatile nature of the relationship.

How others can help

Many of those who have experienced abuse in a marriage find themselves alone and unable to trust those around them. They have been criticized and ridiculed so much that they now doubt themselves and their perceptions. Unsure themselves about their situation, they are afraid to relate their experiences to others who might question, judge, and condemn. They may fear that, if they tell someone, their marriage situation will become public knowledge and their husband will become angrier and more difficult. They desperately need the help of compassionate friends.

Those who stand by watching and wondering are often unsure about how to care. They know that they cannot and should not assume the role of therapist, which only a trained professional should take on. There are, however, many other ways in which help can be offered:

1. Allow the abused person to talk. The greatest gift you can offer someone in this situation is the freedom to talk about the years of mistreatment, the damage to family, and the resulting grief.
2. Learn to listen to what the abused person is saying. Accept and validate her feelings about the experience. She needs to hear that it is okay for her to feel angry, sad, hurt, or afraid.
3. Acknowledge the abuse. Recognize that abuse occurred and that she endured years of insults. Do not judge what she tells you. She needs to have her perceptions respected without judgement or condemnation.
4. Avoid easy answers such as, "God will see you through this," or "All things work together for good." She needs to hear that you care and that you appreciate the severity of her situation. There are no easy answers, and offering any is likely to cause her more shame.
5. Allow her to grieve. She has much to grieve for and needs to share her grief. Allow her to be angry and to express her feelings without being judged. These feelings are normal for a person who has experienced severe abuse, and she needs the freedom to express them in an atmosphere of acceptance.
6. Be available and willing to wait for her to share her grief with you. In order to be able to deal with the pain of abuse, she may have had to withdraw emotionally, and she may even be unable to recognize that she has strong feelings. However, when she is ready to express feelings and to grieve, she will need you to be available to listen.

7. Avoid blaming her for the abuse that has happened.
8. Be available to talk and pray with her, on the phone or in person. It will help to let her talk through her concerns as she processes them.
9. Be available to help with instrumental tasks and child care. If she is depressed and lacking energy, she may need you to help with the children or even with simple tasks like getting groceries.
10. Respect her need for distance. The abused person has erected many defences for self-protection and has developed behaviours that keep other people at arm's length, such as failing to ask when she needs help or being reticent to share her feelings. These might seem unreasonable and you may feel that she is rejecting you or your help. These defences are there because she has needed them in order to cope with the past. Therefore, you will need to be patient during those times when she withdraws or becomes angry at you.
11. Recognize that she is likely to be depressed. Depression is an inevitable part of being abused. If you suspect that she is depressed, you can call your local Distress Centre for assistance in how to relate to her. The following list, drawn from information contained in the American Psychiatric Association (1987) *Diagnostic and statistical manual of mental disorders* (fourth edition, revised), Washington, D.C., outlines some things to look for if you think your friend or relative might be depressed:
    a. Anxiety over activities that most of us do without thinking, such as going to the bank.
    b. Feeling jittery and "on edge."
    c. Tearfulness.
    d. Feelings of hopelessness.

e. Fatigue and loss of energy. Sometimes the fatigue is so severe she may feel unable to get out of bed.

f. Change in appetite, either eating much more or much less than usual.

g. Change in sleeping pattern, either wakening very early or needing to sleep much of the day.

h. Social withdrawal, such as not wanting to attend social gatherings or visit with others.

i. Inability to concentrate.

j. Difficulty making decisions.

k. Physical symptoms such as headaches and backache that are not diagnosed as a specific illness.

l. Diminished interest or pleasure in almost all activities.

m. Feelings of worthlessness.

n. Inability to experience a range of emotions. Individuals may describe feeling numb and unable to experience joy, sadness, etc.

A depressed person may experience many or few of the symptoms listed above. If you note the presence of several of these indicators, you may want to suggest that she see a medical doctor, who might need to prescribe medication to help her through this difficult period. You can suggest that she visit a counsellor to help her work through her pain and develop coping strategies. She may experience vulnerable periods when she feels severely depressed. These often occur when the children go to visit their father, when she is around a healthy family, or after she has experienced a meeting or interaction with her former husband. When these times are severe, she might need professional help.

12. Be aware that she may experience suicidal thoughts. She might say things like "If it were not for the children, I wouldn't want to live" or she may be more direct with a comment like "I have nothing to live for." Do not attempt to deal with these yourself but direct her to a counsellor. Most cities have a Distress Centre and you may need to call them for guidance on how you can assist her to seek help.
13. Let her know that she has coped in a very difficult situation, and tell her that you realize it has been very hard for her to survive. *Do not criticize* her coping behaviours.
14. Allow her the freedom to be angry at God and to question her religion. These may be essential steps in her healing.

The abuser

It is important to recognize that abusive relationships usually involve issues of power and control. The abuser feels the need to maintain control over his family. Perhaps supported by church teachings, he exerts his authority over his wife and children in an effort to maintain his perceived role as head of the family. Melissa Miller (1994) provides an outline of the characteristics of an abusive husband. The following is a summary of her observations:

1. These men tend to have low self-esteem. They are insecure and do not feel good about themselves.
2. They do not have a good network of friends. Often they have no friends and depend upon their wives to form and maintain a social network.
3. They are incapable of establishing intimate relationships in

which they are known by another. Their insecurity prevents them from trusting others.

4. Some individuals use drugs and alcohol. They may use their substance abuse to avoid taking responsibility for their actions.

5. Abusers use denial to minimize the consequences of their actions.

6. Often abusers have difficulty coping with daily stress, and respond to stress by hurting others.

The abusive man is usually a person who has experienced unmet needs in childhood. As a child, he has struggled to survive and has suffered. He does not know what constitutes a healthy relationship and navigates through relationships using power.

The church must become familiar with the characteristics of the abuser in order to identify them, and then to provide help and recommendations for healing. Miller argues that in spite of our stereotypes, abusers are not rough-looking villains; they are our neighbours, our church leaders, our Sunday school teachers. They are capable of good, but abuse their wives, often for reasons of which they are scarcely aware, and sometimes without consciously recognizing the damage they are doing. The church community must recognize abusers for who they are and offer them a place to heal and resources to help them repent and turn from their sin.

Conclusion

When all factors are considered, it is evident that religious perspectives can contribute to the decision to tolerate abuse, but that they do not cause it. The roots of abuse lie in the early experiences of both the abuser and the abused. The individuals discussed in this book are Christians who experienced marital relationships that lacked the nurture and respect of a healthy marriage. These women depended on legalistic religious teachings to give them guidance when their relationships foundered. Their religion did not cause the abuse. Rather, when they confronted the abuse, their trust in God became a source of courage. Healing comes from recognizing the abuse, grieving the losses, and embracing a God who loves and cares for his children. Healing is sometimes a lengthy and difficult process, but it is one worth enduring, if only because it leads to freedom from the abuse and a new and better life.

Chapter Eleven

Shirley

*"I wanted to lie down
and let the life seep out of me."*

I was married to Dennis for sixteen years. I can hardly believe it now, but we had a lot of good times together, and he gave me four children I dearly love.

I came from a religious family. We attended church and said prayers in school. I was the third of five children. I felt very alone in the family. My older brother and sister were quite close, and my two younger sisters got along with each other. I was quite a tomboy, and I always seemed to be the odd one out. We were quite poor, and my father worked hard to support us. He was a very controlling man, and my mother always did as he said. I don't think she was a very happy person. She put a lot of energy into raising the children by doing physical things for us, but I never got to know her as a real person because she was distant and stern. My family valued independence and taught us kids that we must never lean on anyone or turn to others for help. "Don't air your dirty laundry in front of others," my parents would say. We also did not air our dirty laundry in the family. Instead, we had to hide our feelings and thoughts, and the result was that we were very distant from each other. Acceptance and approval were conditional upon how we behaved.

As far back as I remember I was very unhappy, and as I grew older I felt a deep grieving sense of isolation. I knew that inside me there was someone crying to get out and be accepted. I just wanted to feel loved. My parents cared for us, but they were cold and distant and too busy to play and spend time with us.

My family placed a value on growing up and finding a spouse. My mother told us that the most important thing for a girl was to grow up and find a husband with a steady job, who could support her. I felt inadequate and wondered if any man would be interested in someone like me.

When I was about nineteen I met Dennis, who was also from a religious family. He lacked any career aspirations and had no money. I suppose he was a bit of a rebel, and I liked that. What drew me to Dennis was the fact that he really seemed to care about me. We got married the next year, when I was twenty. We attended a church during the first year of our marriage, but Dennis criticized the people, the pastor, and the services. Going to church was an ordeal because he was so negative. I believed in God, but he was a God who was just "out there" somewhere; so it wasn't terribly important to attend church.

I soon became pregnant with my eldest daughter, and just after she was born, Dennis started getting angry with me. He wanted all my attention and got jealous when he saw me feeding Marla or holding her. He showed no concern for my health or tiredness. When he got angry over little things, he took his anger out on me by calling me names, putting me down, or threatening to leave me. Sometimes the comments seemed insignificant.

He said things like, "I'll call you at 3:00 to make sure you're home and not out cheating on me" or "How come Marla stinks?

I suppose you can't get your lazy butt in gear to change her."
Sometimes he joked in front of other people, like the time when
the plumber came to fix the leaky taps. Dennis said to the
plumber, "My wife is such a terrible housekeeper that she can't
even turn a tap off properly. Why don't you take her home with
you? I'll take a beer for her. That's all she's worth."

It took all my energy to look after Marla, but I believed
that, if we had more children, Dennis would get to be less jealous. In the next seven years I had three more children, and all I
did was look after the children and run the house. I tried to
meet my needs through the children. If I raised them well, I
might be respected. The sense of fulfillment and achievement I
got from raising them helped to compensate for the lack of love
and care from Dennis. We were very poor, and after the fourth
and last child arrived, things became even worse financially.

Although Dennis only left the house to go to work, at home
he was very distant, sitting by himself and rarely talking to me
or the kids. He had no close friends and no interests; so all he
did was sit around, watch TV, and criticize me. He would tell
me I was stupid and only good for one thing. He told me people did not like me and that I'd never have any friends.
Sometimes he would go several days without speaking to me.
He'd send messages through the kids. When he was really mad,
he said things like, "You're a terrible wife. I don't know why I
married you. I should be shacked up with a beautiful broad, not
stuck here with you." I told myself that at least he did not hit
me, and that the things he said didn't matter — you know, "sticks
and stones will break your bones but names will never hurt you."

Sometimes he said little things, and I didn't know if he was
joking; so I joked back, and this made him really angry. He said
other things such as, "Hey, Sidney, do you know your mother
hasn't cooked a good meal for three months?" or "I can't let

you decide what colour paint to put on the basement wall because you can't see straight." These seemed like such little things, but each comment was like putting a nail to my heart and pounding it in. I prayed and asked God to help me know how to respond to Dennis. I blamed myself and thought that, if I were a better wife, Dennis would value me.

My parents criticized my choice of husband and my parenting skills. Resentfully they offered some financial and practical help, which seemed to be a reminder that in their eyes I was a failure. In order to shut out the pain, I focused on my children. I withdrew from everyone except the kids. Dennis had convinced me that I was so bad a person and wife that I was not worthy of having friends. I felt so much shame that I had to keep a mask on. When there is a barrier, people sense it and back off. I kept telling myself, "Protect yourself from letting other people know you. Put on a front. Be a martyr." Everything I did had to be controlled. I did not attend church for many years.

Although I was unhappy, I did not consider leaving the marriage. I believed that you stay in a marriage no matter what, and I also did not think I could ever survive on my own. The responsibility of raising four children alone seemed overwhelming. During the first ten years of the marriage I kept believing that things could get better. I looked for the good in Dennis. I could see that he did not mistreat the kids. It was only me he picked on.

We moved twice so that Dennis could get a better job. I thought that a new life would give hope and a chance for the kids. Instead, these moves put a terrible strain on our relationship. Dennis's criticism of me grew worse. He would tell the children, I was an unfit mother and that I was not good for them. I kept trying to be good enough and trying to be strong for everyone. Eventually I thought I was going insane. I wanted to be dead. I couldn't even pay attention to the children.

My brother and sisters were living in different parts of the country; so I did not talk to them much. My older sister lived on the west coast, and she phoned about once a month because she knew things were difficult. When I confided in her, she usually told me to try harder and be more feminine. I wanted to trust her more, but our conversations left me feeling condemned and inadequate.

I desperately needed strength. I felt so weary, so tired all the time. Sometimes I went through the day completely spaced out. I don't know how I managed to work part-time and raise the kids. There were many times when I wanted to lie down and let the life seep out of me. It would be so much easier. But then there were the children — I had to carry on and keep things together for the children. There were many days when I could not muster the energy to go to work; so I stayed in bed and mourned for all the things that had not worked out — for the marriage, the children, and the many dreams I had of having a happy home to raise my kids in.

I prayed and asked God to help me understand the pain of my life. It was on one of these days when I experienced a sort of encounter with God. I was at home by myself and all the kids were at school. Suddenly I felt God there, caring for me and giving me strength. I knew, at that point, that there is a God and that perhaps he really loves me. I started regular church attendance. It was hard, though. Dennis was not interested in attending church, and he mocked me. He refused to help me get the kids ready for church each Sunday, and by the time I got there, I was so exhausted I could hardly take in any of the service.

The people I met at the church were kind, but I kept my distance for several months. One day my son's Sunday school teacher approached me and said she was concerned about Jeffrey's swearing. I guess I was at the end of my rope because I just burst into tears and told her that life was very hard. I did not tell her about Dennis, but I let her know that things were bad at home. This lady introduced me to a couple of other ladies. They showed concern and asked questions in a loving way that encouraged me to trust them with some of the hurt and pain in my life. I told them I felt ashamed of my marriage and ashamed of the way I was being treated. These people were not judgemental; they accepted me and prayed for me.

Gradually I disclosed more and more about the abuse and discovered that I was not rejected. They seemed to understand and they showed compassion. As I became more honest about the abuse, I realized that the pain was too deep for me or anyone else to fix, and I turned more and more to God. Realizing how destructive the relationship had been and how it had affected the children brought even more pain, but gradually I came alive and found hope. I could not believe it had taken so long to see the truth.

I got involved in church activities and enjoyed spending time with my new friends. I still did not consider leaving Dennis because I was terrified of not making it alone, of not being capable, not being the parent the children needed, of the financial consequences. The terrible marriage was at least familiar, and I was afraid of what I did not know. At some point, a woman from the church talked about how she had been seeing a counsellor, and I recognized that I had to do the same. The counselling was very helpful in getting me to see the truth of my upbringing and marriage.

Eventually I reached a point where I knew I had to get out. Dennis was becoming more horrible. Two of the children were being difficult in school, reacting there to the turmoil at home.

The counsellor supported my decision to separate, and so did the minister at the church I was attending. I received lots of support from my friends at church, who helped me move my stuff, cared for the younger kids, offered money and food, and prayed for me.

Dennis tried to persuade me to go back. Several times he came to my work and created a scene in front of my boss. I rented a basement suite from a man in the church, and Dennis came over there a lot, begging me to go back. After so many years of telling me I was a terrible wife and how much he wanted to get rid of me, Dennis could not deal with the fact that I had left him. I felt sorry for Dennis because I really believed he could not cope with life unless I took care of him. We had many long conversations where we talked about the marriage and the problems. Dennis never took responsibility for his behaviour. He always had an explanation or a reason for what happened. He told me things did not happen the way I remembered, and he convinced me that my perceptions were wrong. I was such a zombie for so many years that perhaps I did not remember things the way they really were. Perhaps I exaggerated, just like Dennis said.

This was a very difficult time for me, because I kept waffling back and forth. On one level, I knew that the marriage was very destructive, and, on the other hand, I felt sorry for Dennis and wanted to make every effort to save the family. I lived on my own for four months, but during that time I felt more bound to Dennis than I had for years. I was consumed with thoughts of the marriage, the family, and the fear that maybe I was doing the wrong thing.

In the end I moved back with Dennis in order to try it again. The kids all blamed me for wrecking their lives. They were glad to move back with Dennis. I only lasted about six months.

The critical comments and ridicule started right away and soon became too much to endure. The day I moved back in, Dennis told the kids I'd wasted money by moving out and I'd ruined their schooling by dragging them across town.

I went back to my church friends and asked them to pray for me. I knew I had to leave, and I was sure it would take a greater effort this time because I had already tried and failed. When I finally left, it was not as bad as I expected. I was definitely more prepared, and mentally I was ready to go. Something changed inside my head. I don't know if it was God or if I gradually became more aware of the destruction, but something gave me the strength to move into an apartment with the two younger kids, while Marla and Jeffrey stayed with their dad.

Once I was out of the marriage, it was like coming alive. I spent a lot of time with my friends, and attended two Bible study groups. The older kids came over and babysat the young ones. I got so much support from friends at church that it was easy to go to church potlucks and be involved with the choir. Someone even gave me a car and others brought furniture. The next two years were not easy, as I had to work hard to make ends meet. Sometimes I felt very tired, but each morning when I got up, I looked forward to the day.

I realize that I am a very sociable person and need to be around people. I still have grief and sadness for what might have been. There is a sense of loss, especially for the kids. I had kept so many things from them and had lied so often, saying that things were fine when it was obvious that they were in a terrible mess, that now the children find it hard to trust me. It will be hard work to build new relationships with them based on honesty and acceptance.

I believe the first turning point for me was when I got close to God. It awakened something inside me that showed me my worth and helped me see how bad the marriage was. The second turning point came when, through counselling, I realized I was too weary and weak to parent my children. I loved my children and I never wanted to do anything to hurt them. When I saw how badly they were affected by the marriage, by Dennis's put-downs of me, and by my own inability to parent, I knew I had to make a change.

Chapter Twelve

Where Are They Today?

The women whom you have met in these pages all made the choice to terminate an abusive marriage. After many years of trying to effect change themselves and praying for God to change things for them, they decided that the only way out was divorce. This is not the right choice for everyone. Some women continue to work at their marriages, believing that God desires them to stay. Others take strides to terminate the abuse and find that their spouses are willing to change. It is not for us to judge another's decision, but only to offer a safe place for the abused woman to tell her story and be heard. The stories you have read document the lives of Christian women who loved God but married controlling and abusive men. What happened to these women? Where they are today?

Lily remarried and worked together with her husband for a number of years. She was active in their church's music ministry and remains involved with community groups and services where she cares for "fellow sufferers." She experiences ongoing healing and feels confident that, by sharing her story, others can find hope to heal their own pain. Her three children have been involved in counselling and are slowly recovering. The trauma of living their childhood with an angry father and their current lack of contact with him have left them with many issues to resolve. Considering the impact of domestic abuse over such an extended period of time, Lily believes her own diligent efforts to pursue healing at any cost present a model of on-going change for her family and friends. She credits her "creative compassionate God" with helping her family continue recovering from deep wounds.

Marie, the woman who endured two bad marriages, has never remarried. She works for a large corporation where she holds an important position. Marie involves herself with church responsibilities and attends Bible studies because she still finds that the support of other Christians is a necessary part of her recovery. She has discovered a passion for travel and has several travelling companions who also share her passion. She has experienced much healing and now enjoys the freedom of being herself, although she believes that her healing journey remains a dynamic process that will never end. Marie's children still struggle with their wounds and experience difficulty in their relationships. She agonizes over the harm they experienced and still struggles with her guilt, constantly taking this to God and asking him to protect and heal her children.

Barbara has remained single. Her debts now paid off, she lives alone and works at a prestigious company. Barbara has developed a passion for volunteer work along with her other passion, singing. She reports that she is very happy with her life. Her children are now adults, and all except one seem to be healing from their pain. Initially Caroline, the daughter so rejected by her father, seemed to be surviving her trauma with few scars. As she entered adulthood, however, Caroline began to face the rejection and to deal with her father's treatment of her mother. Barbara fears that for Caroline healing will take a long time.

Opal continued with her recovery program of attending support groups and pursuing activities that brought her joy. She married a "wonderful man" with whom she shares a nurturing relationship. She works part-time in her husband's business. Active in the church, Opal and her husband run support groups for those who struggle with life's issues and are involved with a ministry to children. Opal still grieves for her children and mourns the lost years when she was unable to truly care for them. Her children have very little contact with their father and are coping with their losses in different ways, some by distancing and others by seeking to understand their family issues. They are all in different stages of recovery, and Opal intercedes daily for their healing.

Although Shirley has experienced tremendous healing and is now happily remarried, she has found that her journey since the divorce has been in some ways more difficult than her first marriage. Her second marriage has not been the fairy tale of which she had dreamed. It has presented its own challenges, revolving around the couple's combined family. But confronting the challenges has led to deeper healing. "The difference is, I'm dealing with the pain of reality, not the pain of denial. It's the pain of facing myself, the deep hurts, disappointments, longings, and fears." She is active in the church community and enjoys a diverse array of interests, hobbies, and friendships. She relies heavily on prayer and her relationship with God to carry her through each day. "I find myself not basking on the mountaintop, but hanging on to God for the marriage, for our children, and for our hope and future."

Appendix A

Boundaries

A boundary is a concrete or imaginary line that indicates a perimeter. A personal boundary is like a fence, and just as a fence tells us the boundary of a field or yard, so a personal boundary separates what is me and mine from what is not about me. The skin is a physical boundary that keeps all the muscles, tendons, blood, and bone inside our bodies. An emotional boundary, although invisible, keeps our thoughts and feelings contained inside it. They are distinctly our own. We respond to the world in ways that are unique to our individual perceptions, histories, and values. We have our distinctive likes and dislikes, loves and hates, that either nurture or destroy us. A boundary is violated when someone gets into our personal space and tells us how we should think and feel, what to like and dislike, and what to believe. When the boundary is violated, the other person may gain control of us.

Boundaries can be classified as flexible, weak, or rigid. The ideal boundary is one that is flexible enough to allow the good things in and keep the bad out. An individual with this kind of boundary is able to say no to those things that she does not desire and yes to the things she does. As Ann Katherine states (1991, p. 8) "If our boundaries are intact, we have a sense of well-being ... we can determine to exclude meanness and hostility and let in affection, kindness, and positive regard."

Some people's boundaries are too weak. These people allow others to tell them how they should feel, what they should do, and how they should behave. These are the people who have difficulty saying no when they are asked to do something. Others have boundaries that are too rigid. These people keep a safe distance from the world. They do not risk being vulnerable with others and disclose very little about themselves.

Adults' boundaries have developed out of childhood experiences. When a child's boundary is respected, parents honour the child's feelings and thoughts and respect the child's likes and dislikes. The child is affirmed for who he or she is. In such cases the boundary that develops is likely to have the flexibility of a fence with a gate in it. The gate can be opened and closed to allow certain things in and others out. A flexible boundary around an individual can be relaxed to allow in nurturing care, but it can also be raised to keep out abusive words.

Parents often violate a child's boundaries by telling the child she does not like something that is very special to her or telling her she should not think in a certain way. The child is not free to say no or explore for herself. A child whose boundaries have not been respected may grow up to be an adult with either weak or rigid boundaries. Adults with weak boundaries depend on the approval of others for their sense of well-being. They are likely to be unable to say no for fear of being rejected or disliked. Families in which boundaries are weak often make unclear distinctions between generations and between family members.

In some families, parents are distant from the child and fail to provide affection and acceptance. Such parents often have rigid boundaries, sharing little of themselves with their offspring. According to Katherine (1991), a lack of parental warmth and attention results in an individual's experience of stunted emotional development. When this occurs, the child's needs for significance, affection, and belonging remain unmet. The child fails to learn healthy ways to interact with others or establish relationships. As adults, these individuals are likely to fear intimacy and erect walls around themselves to protect them from intrusion and to keep the self safe. When boundaries become walls, they are too rigid. They prevent a person from getting close to others and keep the individual closed off from intimacy. Families where boundaries are rigid keep themselves walled off from others. These families do not allow children to bring friends home, do not invite people to visit, and fail to let the children visit other families.

Knowing ourselves — this is me or mine; this is not me or mine — gives us freedom, helps us to feel secure, and encourages us to take responsibility for ourselves. When we do not know what is ours and what is not, we are confused. It is like playing soccer on a field with no white line around it. The players would wonder where they can kick the ball and when a throw-in needs to be taken. When the field is marked with clear lines, the players are secure in knowing their limits.

To have healthy boundaries, we must get to know ourselves and be able to differentiate between our own self and others. Therefore a healthy boundary allows an individual to decide what to tolerate, when to say yes and when it is time to halt unwanted behaviours and to say no. Ann Katherine posits that a person's emotional health is directly related to the health of her boundaries.

A discussion of boundaries would not be complete without reference to the difference between enmeshment and intimacy.

According to Ann Katherine, enmeshment might feel like intimacy; however, intimacy develops when individuals get to know each other well, accept each other's differences and shortcomings, and still continue to love and care for one another. In a loving relationship, individuals have flexible boundaries and are aware of who they are. They do not try to be like each other or to make the partner like themselves or someone else. Enmeshment, by contrast, occurs when partners attempt to think and feel the same. Each tries to be like the other, unable to accept or even recognize uniqueness in each other's differences. Often one partner in particular will give up being herself or himself and try to be what the other wants. In the resulting relationship, boundaries are weak and neither partner knows where he or she ends and the other begins.

Appendix B

Family Rules and Roles

Every family is unique, having its own structure. Its structure is distinguished from that of other families by the number of members, whether one or both parents are present, whether extended family live in. Members have their distinctive roles. For example, they meet the family's needs by performing such tasks as working to provide money for food and shelter, caring for children, preparing meals, and maintaining the home. In a troubled family the structure is falling apart. The fear of family break-up forces family members to select a role or combination of roles that they can each play in an attempt to keep the structure together. Children tend to fall into these roles very early in their development, and as they become comfortable with the role, it becomes a part of the child. As the child grows up, he or she will continue playing the same role in other relationships, even after leaving home.

Dr. Robert Hemfelt, Dr. Frank Minirth, and Dr. Paul Meier (1989) describe different roles that children play within the troubled family:

The hero keeps the family going and picks up the slack. He or she takes care of the younger children, looks after the parents, keeps the household going, gets good grades, and generally is a model child.

The scapegoat is usually the black sheep, the one who is blamed when things go wrong. He or she gets attention by being labelled the difficult child.

The mascot is the family clown who earns attention by being cute or funny, lightening the darkness with wit and humour. This family member is often the saddest, believing that it is never permissible to be troubled, and feeling the pressure to always make light of situations by joking.

The lost child is the nice child who follows the rules and generally fades into the wood work. He or she often plays alone and asks for nothing. This child forms little sense of self because she is given limited attention and fails to experience affirmation and acknowledgement. Therefore she does not really know who he or she is.

These roles appear in most families, but they are heightened in troubled families, where individuals become prisoners, and the children are unable to change their ways of relating.

According to Hemfelt, Minirth, and Meier, a number of other roles have been observed to occur only in troubled families. These roles prevent family members from developing intimacy with others. If people cannot be real, they cannot develop intimacy. When people play roles, they are prevented from being authentic.

The enabler. Most family members in troubled families are enablers. The enablers are those who allow the trouble to continue by utilizing such behaviours as protecting one another from the truth and horror of the situation, or keeping secrets.

The placater tries to promote harmony. He or she is a born negotiator who knows what to say to soothe another person, minimize the conflict, and reduce family friction.

The martyr sacrifices time, energy, and happiness to try to get the family running smoothly. The martyr denies the self in order to keep others functioning.

The rescuer is the one who intervenes and tries to fix the situation. He or she will take over tasks that should be the responsibility of others and, in so doing, allows others to avoid taking responsibility for themselves. This person's goal is to fix other family members, to clean up the damage, and to minimize the mess.

The persecuter takes no responsibility for the family situation. He or she blames others, points out their shortcomings, and is generally unpleasant.

The victim expresses intense self-pity and blames the circumstances on the shortcomings of others. Individuals who play this role believe that their suffering is undeserved and that, if other people changed, harmony and happiness would follow.

The roles people play are reinforced by family rules that make it difficult for individuals to give up their roles. Troubled families often exercise rules that result in family members being unable to relate authentically to one another. Behaviours that fall within the rules are considered safe. Those that lie outside the rules are considered dangerous, and if family members break the rules, there are serious consequences, such as anger or abuse.

Claudia Black (1981) identified three rules that members of alcoholic families use to survive. These can also be identified in many troubled families where alcohol is not a problem:

1. **Don't talk.** This rule tells children to speak when spoken to, keep quiet, and stay out of the way. Children learn to keep the family secrets and not to talk about concerns or observations either inside or outside the family. If they talk about issues, they are told that the issues are merely in their own imaginations.

2. **Don't trust.** Children learn this rule by seeing promise after promise broken. Since it is safer not to believe in others, they learn to be on guard and always hold part of themselves back from others, avoiding intimacy and giving something only when there is certainty of getting something in return.

3. **Don't feel.** This rule teaches children not to express feelings because to do so shows weakness and gives others power over them. It is easier not to feel.

To Black's rules we can add these:

4. **Don't think.** Adults are right and children wrong. Children are taught to obey without question. They learn never to evaluate, reason, judge, or question. When children are oppressed in this way, they use their ability to dream and imagine as a form of escape, not as a method of creative

growth. Children who grow up with this rule are likely to become adults who are always right and fail to listen to their own children.

5. **Don't see.** This rules teaches children to do only what parents say and not what they do. Children question their own reality because they learn that what they see is not really what there is. They are encouraged to act older than their age, be serious, take on adult responsibility and cause no trouble. Fun and play are limited.

6. **Be thankful.** Children are encouraged to be thankful for their parents' sacrifices. Children have this forced upon them when they have no idea what they are supposed to be thankful for.

These rules keep families bound in troubled ways of relating. Family members are unable to relate to each other out of the way they really feel and think. Therefore, they remain limited by behaviours that are acceptable to the family. They are unable to explore other ways of being in the world and stay trapped in their respective roles.

Post-Traumatic Stress Disorder

The essential feature of this disorder is the development of characteristic symptoms following a psychologically distressing event that is outside the range of usual human experience (i.e., outside the range of such common experiences as simple bereavement, chronic illness, business losses, and marital conflict). The stressor producing this syndrome would be markedly distressing to almost anyone, and the stress is usually experienced with intense fear, terror, and helplessness. The characteristic symptoms involve re-experiencing the traumatic event, avoidance of stimuli associated with the event, numbing of general responsiveness, and increased arousal. The diagnosis is not made if the disturbance lasts less than one month.

The most common traumata involve either a serious threat to one's life or physical integrity; a serious threat or harm to one's children, spouse, or other close relatives and friends; sudden destruction of one's home or community; and seeing another person who has recently been, or is being, seriously injured or killed as the result of an accident or physical violence. In some cases the trauma may be learning about a serious threat or harm to a close friend or relative; *e.g.*, that one's child has been kidnapped, tortured, or killed.

The trauma may be experienced alone (*e.g.*, rape or assault) or in the company of groups of people (*e.g.*, military combat). Stressors producing this disorder include natural disasters (*e.g.*, floods, earthquakes), accident disasters (*e.g.*, car accidents with serious physical injury, airplane crashes, large fires, collapse of physical structures), or deliberately caused disasters (*e.g.*, bombing, torture, death camps). Some stressors frequently produce the disorder (*e.g.*, torture) and others produce it only occasionally (*e.g.*, natural disasters or car accidents). Sometimes there is a concomitant physical component of the trauma, which may even involve direct damage to the central nervous system (*e.g.*, malnutrition, head injury). The disorder is apparently more severe and longer lasting when the stressor is of human design.

The traumatic event can be re-experienced in a variety of ways. Commonly the person has recurrent and intrusive recollections of the event or recurrent distressing dreams during which the event is re-experienced. In rare instances, there are dissociative states, lasting from a few seconds to several hours or even days, during which the components of the event are relived and the person behaves as though experiencing the event at that moment. There is often intense psychological distress when the person is exposed to events that resemble an aspect of the traumatic event or that symbolize the traumatic event, such as anniversaries of the event.

A second symptom of post-traumatic stress disorder is persistent avoidance of stimuli associated with it. The person commonly makes deliberate efforts to avoid thoughts or feelings about the traumatic event and about activities or situations that arouse recollections of it. This avoidance of reminders of the trauma may include psychogenic amnesia for an important aspect of the traumatic event.

A third symptom, diminished responsiveness to the external world, referred to as "psychic numbing" or "emotional anesthesia," usually begins soon after the traumatic event. A person may complain of feeling detached or estranged from other people; that he or she has lost the ability to become interested in previously enjoyed activities; or that the ability to feel emotions of any type, especially those associated with intimacy, tenderness, and sexuality, is markedly decreased.

The fourth symptom, increased arousal that was not present before the trauma, includes difficulty falling or staying asleep (recurrent nightmares during which the traumatic event is relived are sometimes accompanied by middle or terminal sleep disturbance), hyper-vigilance, and exaggerated startle response. Some complain of difficulty in concentrating or in completing tasks. Many report changes in aggression. In mild cases, this may take the form of irritability with fear of losing control. In more severe forms, particularly in cases in which the survivor has actually committed acts of violence (as in war veterans), the fear is conscious and pervasive, and the reduced capacity for modulation may express itself in unpredictable explosions of aggressive behaviour or an inability to express angry feelings.

Symptoms characteristic of Post-Traumatic Stress Disorder, or Physiologic Reactivity, are often intensified or precipitated when the person is exposed to situations or activities that resemble or symbolize the original trauma (American Psychiatric Association [1987] *Diagnostic and statistical manual of mental disorders* [third edition, revised]. Washington, D.C., pp. 247–248).

Defence Mechanisms

Ego defences are mechanisms that distort perceptions and help an individual to avoid facing painful experiences. These distortions can be healthy ways for the mind to protect itself from being overwhelmed. When appropriately used, defences can be helpful to block periodic anxiety, such as after a death or traumatic accident. In such cases the defences are only temporary and gradually withdraw with time, allowing the individual to experience the pain that needs to be faced in order to promote healing.

When painful experiences are overwhelming, defences can develop which keep the person from recognizing the seriousness of a situation. In contrast to healthy defences, these do not withdraw over time but become more solidified, thus forming walls that keep the individual from breaking through to healing and wholeness.

There are various defences that the mind creates, such as denial, minimization, and delusion, which distort the perceptions. In addition, suppression and repression enable perceptions to be blocked out completely.

Denial occurs when an individual fails to acknowledge pain and the circumstances surrounding it. The fear of facing memories and experiences is so great that the person uses denial and refuses to admit that there is a problem, or fails to acknowledge the extent of the problem. When individuals are abused, their denial becomes greater, and consequently so does their tolerance for the abuse.

A partner of denial is **minimization**, which involves minimizing the seriousness of a situation in order to make it more acceptable. Many abused individuals tell themselves that the situation is not too bad, or that other people endure circumstances that are far worse. One woman in her second abusive marriage believed, "It was not that bad because the first marriage was much worse."

Rationalization is creating reasons to explain why something is happening. Positing plausible reasons serves to justify remaining in an abusive situation and to distance the horror. Many abused women tell themselves, "This is the way marriage is supposed to be"; "All men act this way, not just my husband"; "He can't help it"; "I must have deserved this"; or "If I were a better wife, this would not happen."

Delusion provides false beliefs that make a situation more palatable. People tolerate painful situations by reframing the pain into positive thoughts, thus blocking out the pain. Some abused individuals believe, "My man is not the type of person who would hurt me badly," or "He's an elder in the church, and he prays so much; he cannot be a bad man." Other women tell themselves that God is allowing the problems to occur because he is preparing them for a specific task. Others believe God is refining the husband because he is going to use their family for a great purpose.

When **suppression** is employed, the individual consciously chooses to forget a trauma in order to block out the pain. **Repression** occurs when an individual is unaware of blocking out memories. Painful incidents are often recalled by people many years after the trauma, and they express surprise at not remembering these.

The Cycle of Violence

Through her work and research with battered women, Lenore Walker (1979) developed a theory of why women stay in marriages that is widely accepted by other experts in the field of family violence. The "Cycle of Violence Theory" describes interpersonal aggression that intensifies in degree and frequency over time and holds the people involved in an established pattern of behaviour.

The Cycle of Violence consists of three phases:

(a) **Tension building** is the phase in which minor incidents of violence may occur along with a buildup of anger. This phase may include verbal put-downs, jealousy, threats, and breaking things, and it may last over an indefinite period of time. Eventually, this phase will escalate to the second phase.

(b) **Acute battering** is the phase in which the major violent outburst occurs. This violence can be seen as the major earthquake, and the episodes during tension building as the foreshocks. Following the second phase, the couple (or family if there are children) will enter the third phase.

(c) **The honeymoon, or loving respite,** is the phase in which the batterer is remorseful and afraid of losing his partner. He may promise anything, beg forgiveness, buy gifts, be effusively communicative with a passion fuelled by guilt, and basically be "the man she fell in love with." Over time there is a change as the batterer externalizes the blame (blames others, primarily his wife) and she internalizes it (blames herself, not him). Information from both men and women indicated that, in many cases, the alleged "honeymoon" was simply a cessation of violence and that, for the abuser, repentance was short-lived (Barnett, O.W., and LaViolette, A.D., 1993). *It Could Happen to Anyone: Why Battered Women Stay.* Newbury Park: Sage, pp. xxii-xxiii).

Appendix F

Recommended Reading

Allender, D.B. *The Wounded Heart: Hope for Adult Survivors of Childhood Sexual Abuse*. Colorado Springs, Colorado: NavPress, 1990.

Alsdurf, J., and P. Alsdurf. *Battered into Submission: The Tragedy of Wife Abuse in the Christian Home*. Downers Grove, Illinois: InterVarsity, 1989.

Barnett, O.W., and A.D. LaViolette. *It Could Happen to Anyone: Why Battered Women Stay*. Newbury Park, CA: SAGE Publications Inc., 1993.

Clark Kroeger, C., and J.R. Beck (ed). *Healing the Hurting*. Grand Rapids, Michigan: Baker Book House, 1998.

Cloud, H., and J. Townsend. *Boundaries: When to Say Yes, When to Say No, To Take Control of Your Life*. Grand Rapids, Michigan: Zondervan, 1992.

Engel, B. *The Emotionally Abused Woman*. New York: Fawcett Columbine, 1990.

Evans, P. *The Verbally Abusive Relationship: How to Recognize It and How to Respond.* Holbrook, Massachusetts: Bob Adams, Inc., 1992.

Fortune, M.M. *Keeping the Faith. Questions and Answers for the Abused Woman.* San Francisco: Harper & Row, 1987.

General Synod of the Anglican Church of Canada. *Violence against Women: Taskforce Report to General Synod.* Toronto: Anglican Book Centre, 1986.

Hemfelt, R., F. Minirth, and P. Meier. *Love is a Choice: Recovery for Codependent Relationships.* Nashville:Thomas Nelson, 1989.

Katherine, A. *Boundaries: Where You End and I Begin.* USA: Simon & Schuster, 1991.

Miller, J.K. *A Hunger for Healing: The Twelve Steps as a Classic Model for Christian Spiritual Growth.* New York: HarperSanFrancisco, 1991.

Nason-Clark, N. *The Battered Wife.* Louisville, Kentucky: Westminster John Knowles Press, 1997.

Radford Ruether, Rosemary. *Christianity and the Making of the Modern Family.* Boston: Beacon Press, 2000.

Radford Ruether, Rosemary. *Sexism and God Talk.* Boston: Beacon Press, 1983, 1993.

Walker, L.E. *The Battered Woman.* New York: Harper & Row, 1979.

References

Allender, D.B. *The Wounded Heart: Hope for Adult Survivors of Childhood Sexual Abuse.* Colorado Springs, Colorado: NavPress, 1990.

Alsdurf, J., and P. Alsdurf. *Battered into Submission: The Tragedy of Wife Abuse in the Christian Home.* Downers Grove, Illinois: InterVarsity, 1989.

Barnett, O.W., and A.D. LaViolette. *It Could Happen to Anyone: Why Battered Women Stay.* Newbury Park, California: SAGE Publications Inc., 1993.

Bass, E., and L. Davis. 1994. *The Courage to Heal.* 3rd ed. New York: Harper and Row.

Black, C. *It Will Never Happen to Me.* Denver: MAC Printing & Publication Division, 1981.

Bowen, M. *Family Therapy in Clinical Practice.* New York: Jason Aronson, 1978.

Bradshaw, J. *Healing the Shame that Binds You.* Deerfield Beach, Florida: Health Communications Inc., 1988.

Brown, J.C., and C.R. Bohn. "For God so loved the world." In *Christianity, Patriarchy and Abuse: A Feminist Critique*, ed. J.C. Brown and C.R. Bohn, 1–30. Cleveland, Ohio: Pilgrim Press, 1989.

Brown, J.C., and R. Parker, R. "Introduction." In *Christianity, Patriarchy and Abuse: A Feminist Critique*, ed. J.C. Brown and C.R. Bohn, xiii–xv. Cleveland, Ohio: Pilgrim Press, 1989.

Butler, Sandra. *Conspiracy of Silence: The Trauma of Incest*. Volcano, California: Volcano Press, 1978, 1996.

Christian Reformed Church. *Agenda for Synod*. Grand Rapids, Michigan, 1992.

Cloud, H., and J. Townsend. *Boundaries: When to Say Yes, When to Say No, To Take Control of Your Life*. Grand Rapids, Michigan: Zondervan, 1992.

Courtois, Christine A. *Healing the Incest Wound: Adult Survivors in Therapy*. New York: Norton, 1998.

Engel, B. *The Emotionally Abused Woman*. New York: Fawcett Columbine, 1990.

Ezell, C. "Power, patriarchy, and abusive marriages." In *Healing the Hurting: Giving Hope and Help to Abused Women*, ed. C. Clark Kroeger and J. R. Beck, 15–39. Grand Rapids, Michigan: Baker Book House, 1998.

Fortune, M.M. "A commentary on religious issues in family violence." Seattle: Center for Prevention of Sexual and Domestic Violence Newsletter, 1980.

————. "The church and domestic violence." *Theology News and Notes*, June 1982.

————. *Keeping the Faith. Questions and Answers for the Abused Woman*. San Francisco: Harper & Row, 1987.

Friel, J., and L. Friel. "Adult children: The secrets of dysfunctional families." Florida: Health Communications Inc., 1988.

General Synod of the Anglican Church of Canada. *Violence against Women: Taskforce Report to General Synod.* Toronto: Anglican Book Centre, 1986.

General Synod of the Anglican Church of Canada. *Handbook.* Toronto: Anglican Book Centre, 2002.

General Synod of the Christian Reformed Church. *Agenda for Synod.* Grand Rapids, Michigan, 1992.

Hemfelt, R., F. Minirth, and P. Meier. *Love Is A Choice: Recovery for Codependent Relationships.* Nashville: Thomas Nelson, 1989.

Herman, Judith. *Trauma and Recovery.* New York: Basic Books, 1992, 1997.

Horton, A.L., M.M. Wilkins, and W. Wright. "Women who ended abuse. What religious leaders and religion did for these victims." In *Abuse and Religion: When Praying Isn't Enough,* ed. A.L. Horton and J.A. Williamson, 253–256. Lexington, Massachusetts: Lexington Books, 1988.

Johnson, D., and J. VanVonderen. *The Subtle Power of Spiritual Abuse: Recognizing and Escaping Spiritual Manipulation and False Spiritual Authority within the Church.* Minneapolis: Bethany House, 1991.

Katherine, A. *Boundaries: Where You End and I Begin.* USA: Simon & Schuster, 1991.

Kaufman-Kennel, M. *The Church: A Roadblock for Battered Women.* Mennonite Central Committee Women's Concerns Report (Sept. to Oct.): 5–7, 1987.Maltz, Wendy. *Sexual Healing Journey.* Harper Collins: New York, 1991.

Martin, G.L. *Counseling for Family Violence and Abuse.* Dallas: Word Publishing, 1987. Mennonite Central Committee.

The Purple Packet: Domestic Violence Taskforce. Kitchener, Ontario: Mennonite Central Committee, 1991.

Miller, M. *Family Violence: The Compassionate Church Responds.* Waterloo, Ontario: Herald Press, 1994.

Nason-Clark, N. *The Battered Wife.* Louisville, Kentucky: Westminster John Knowles Press, 1997.

Nouwen, H. *Wounded Healer: Ministry in Contemporary Society.* New York: Doubleday, 1972.

Pressman, B. "Treatment of wife abuse: The case for feminist therapy." In *Intervening with Assaulted Women: Current Theory, Research, and Practice* (21–46), ed. B. Pressman, G. Cameron, and M. Rothery. New Jersey: Lawrence Erlbaum Associates, 1989.

Rogers, S.A. *Experiences of Women with Strong Religious Convictions who Endured and Terminated Abusive Marital Relationships.* Calgary, Alberta: University of Calgary, 1994.

Smedes, L.B. *Mere Mortality.* Grand Rapids, Michigan: Eerdmans, 1983.

Tanner, A. *Treasures of Darkness: Struggling with Separation and Divorce in the Church.* Toronto: Anglican Book Centre, 1990.

Walker, L.E. *The Battered Woman.* New York: Harper & Row, 1979.

Whipple, V. "Counseling battered women from fundamentalist churches." *Journal of Marital and Family Therapy* 13 (3): 251–258, 1987.

Wildman White, A. "The silent killer of Christian marriages." In *Healing the Hurting: Giving Hope and Help to Abused Women*, ed. C. Clark Kroeger and J.R. Beck. Grand Rapids, Michigan: Baker Book House, 1998.

Path Books
A LIGHT TO MY PATH

We hope that you have enjoyed reading this Path Book. For more information about Path Books, please visit our website at **www.pathbooks.com**. If you have comments or suggestions about Path Books, please write to us at publisher@pathbooks.com.

Other Path Books

God with Us: The Companionship of Jesus in the Challenges of Life by Herbert O'Driscoll. In thirty-three perceptive meditations, Herbert O'Driscoll considers the challenges of being human, searches key events in the life of Jesus, and discovers new vitality and guidance for our living. He shows us how the healing wisdom and power of Jesus' life can transform our own lives today.
1-55126-359-9 $18.95

The Habit of Hope: In a Changing and Uncertain World by William Hockin. Wise and friendly guidance to help people living in an age of confusion and change to transform personal experience in the light of biblical story.
1-55126-325-4 $14.95

Passiontide: A Novel by Brian Pearson. In the midst of a spirited West Coast people, David, an Anglican priest, veers into the tangled realms of love and passion, and stares even into the jaws of death. This unpredictable pilgrimage of the soul makes no guarantees and offers no safe haven. He will never be the same again.
1-55126-350-5 $24.95

Practical Prayer: Making Space for God in Everyday Life by Anne Tanner. A richly textured presentation of the history, practices, and implications of Christian prayer and meditation to help people live a rewarding life in a stressful world. *1-55126-321-1 $18.95*

Meditation CD: *1-55126-348-3, $18.95*
Audio cassette: 1-55126-349-1, $16.95
Leader's Guide: 1-55126-347-5, $18.95

Prayer Companion: A Treasury of Personal Meditation by Judith Lawrence. A personal prayer resource providing gems for daily living, meditation, and prayer. A friendly companion to those searching for greater meaning in everyday experience. *1-55126-319-X $18.95*

*Available from your local bookstore or
Anglican Book Centre, phone 1-800-268-1168
or write 600 Jarvis Street, Toronto, ON M4Y 2J6*